Make Me Your Choice

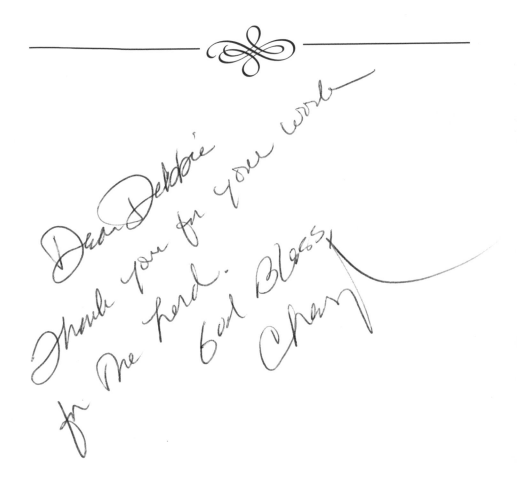

Dear Debbie,
Thank you for your work
for the Lord.
God Bless,
Cheryl

Make Me Your Choice

COMPELLING PERSONAL STORIES
OF STRUGGLE AND HEALING FROM THOSE
WHO HAVE HAD, OR DEALT WITH ABORTION

Cheryl Chew

DESTINY IMAGE® PUBLISHERS, INC.

P.O. Box 310, Shippensburg, PA 17257-0310

*"Speaking to the Purposes of God for this Generation
and for the Generations to Come."*

ISBN 10: 0-7684-2372-4
ISBN 13: 978-0-7684-2372-3

For Worldwide Distribution,
Printed in the U.S.A.

1 2 3 4 5 6 7 8 9 10 11 / 09 08 07 06

This book and all other Destiny Image, Revival Press, Mercy Place, Fresh Bread, Destiny Image Fiction, and Treasure House books are available at Christian bookstores and distributors worldwide.

For a U.S. bookstore nearest you, call **1-800-722-6774.**
For more information on foreign distributors, call **717-532-3040.**
Or reach us on the Internet at:
www.destinyimage.com

DEDICATION

From my heart to yours
This book is lovingly dedicated
To every man and woman who
has had to make a choice.

To all our future generations,
Who are our children,
Our heritage,
Our hope.

To my four beautiful children:
John
David
Mark
Stephanie.

ENDORSEMENT

Cheryl Chew, the author of this book, was a longtime member of Melodyland, a mega-church in Anaheim, California that I pastored for 38 years. I find Cheryl to be an outstanding example of God's plan for our lives. Cheryl excels in character, integrity, and leadership qualities. A gifted teacher and successful businesswoman, Cheryl speaks at many events in Southern California. The perplexing problems in this book are dateless. Courageously, the women have told their stories with amazing transparency. Lornah Stump who shares her story, was also a Melodylander and headed our Ladies' Ministry. Lornah taught many series of classes and was in demand at ladies conferences across America. My wife, Allene, and I esteem both ladies as role models in values for today's world. It's not your choice, it's God's choice. However complex, a life has a right to live. Planned or unplanned, life is priceless. It cannot be terminated as a "biological blunder." Even Mary, the mother of Jesus, had an unplanned birth, but God fulfilled His plan. The young, unmarried maiden faced desperate decisions and encountered chaotic circumstances. Just as Mary never crumbled under social pressures, women of our millennium can find the same supernatural strength to face challenging crises.

PASTOR RALPH WILKERSON

TABLE OF CONTENTS

FOREWORD

There is no greater selfishness than the abortion of a human fetus for the sake of convenience. There is no greater tragedy than abortion. It robs life of its essence and denies the future its value. Abortion is the ignorance of responsibility and the denial of obligation. Abortion is self-comfort at the expense of fruitfulness, because all abortion sacrifices responsibility.

The abortion of potential condemns the future. This reality has caused the development of an entire discipline of science. Ecology and environmental studies, as these areas of concern are called, build their premises on the word "extinction," which means "the termination of the potential force within creation to fulfill itself."

It is amazing that man, with all his attempts to minimize the abortion of various species in the animal and plant kingdoms by investing billions of dollars to protect animals, plants, forests, and the ozone layer, has neglected to prioritize the position of human beings in the scheme of things. While man fights to protect whales, owls, trees, and fish, he also battles for the right to terminate human babies. Perhaps the situation might improve if every doctor who performs this tragic operation would be reminded before each abortion procedure that the opportunity to perform this surgery is possible only because his/her mother did not abort him/her.

The abortion issue is, therefore, not just the problem of the taking of a life, though that is the fatal end result. Even more so, abortion is the destruction of potential. The abortion of a child is the denial of destiny. Abortion is the murdering of the future. Abortion is the death of a divine deposit and the suffocating of a providential investment.

More than 43 million babies are aborted every year around the world. Can you imagine how many geniuses, philosophers, and those who were born to solve many of the world's problems today have been victims of the knife of some abortionist? Thank God for the mothers of Nelson Mandela, John F. Kennedy, Martin Luther King, Jr., Rosa Parks, and Mother Theresa—mothers who chose not to abort their children.

Suppose the mother of Moses had aborted him rather than choosing to fight for his life? Could you imagine if Mary had aborted Jesus Christ? In such a case she would have killed the Savior of the world. Truly there is not a greater tragedy than the abortion of a baby. It is man's ultimate manifestation of his base nature; it is man's lowest act of self-hatred.

I am so grateful that Cheryl Chew has written what I consider an overdue masterpiece. *Make Me Your Choice* is one of the most profound, yet simple discourses on the subject of abortion and lays out a logical, sensitive, compassionate approach to a very delicate subject. Her personalized presentation will draw you into the private world of the womb and allow you to hear the heart, not just the heartbeat, of the helpless, and capture the quiet feelings of a human being in the embryonic state.

I am moved deeply by this book and challenge every reasonable, civilized human being to take the time to read these pages. This book has the potential to save millions of lives and perhaps protect generations from our self-centered culture.

I am proud to be associated with this work and give it two thumbs up. Read on and discover the true value of life and our responsibility and obligation to protect and preserve it. Read it with the awareness that you are only able to do so because your mother "made you her choice."

DR. MYLES E. MUNROE
Pastor and Author
Nassau, Bahamas

PREFACE

From My Heart to Yours

Sometimes we wonder if what we say or do is noticed by others and we may wonder what the effect and reaction of our words and actions will be in the lives of others. Writing this book was very difficult for me in that I had to share my life and my past, and I worried a great deal about what other people will think of me.

When I told my mother that I was writing this book, she voiced her concerns and said, "Everyone will know about you!" Being conflicted about what other people may think about us often causes us to be silent. However, I cannot remain silent any longer because I do know what God thinks about me and how much He loves me and you!

I hope this book will enlighten you with regard to the reasons why some of us made the choice of abortion. Please do not judge us (we have already condemned ourselves with our guilt and shame), but love us and help us to overcome our pain and anguish. My heart goes out to those who are now standing at the doorway of choice, and I pray that this book will help you to make the right choice—that you will keep the beautiful precious gift of life within you!

When I receive letters like the following, I know I've made the right choice by being silent no more, for to remain silent about such important life issues causes one to wither within.

Dear Cheryl,

I just wanted to let you know the feelings of my heart. Sharing your life's past with me has opened my feelings to all women and men who have experienced the choice of abortion.

I really never thought about the pain one feels because it was their choice, till I saw the pain in your eyes and heard the remorse in your voice and how your life became a real living hell.

I experienced two planned pregnancies that ended in miscarriages. I spoke with and shared my pain and grief with other couples as I questioned why this had to happen. How sad and terrible we felt. We told ourselves it wasn't fair and it was not our choice. We were feeling sorry for ourselves.

I was ignorant with regard to the facts and life situations concerning why one would choose an abortion.

However, I've learned that, we have something in common—a great loss and pain, and the same questions: What happens to them? Where are our babies now?

I feel so bad that I once had such a narrow outlook concerning the feelings of others. One's loss through one's choice and one's loss through no choice of one's own are both very painful.

All losses hurt and bring great sorrow. However, sorrow serves a sacred purpose. It is the road to faith. Sorrow gives one a new perspective on life. It's often through great sadness that our true greatness emerges. The fruits of faith fall from the tree of sorrow.

Now you have finally finished your book that you began 10 years ago. I'm sure it will help many people who have experienced the same situation come to terms with their choices and start the healing process they need so desperately.

Your book will help parents to be more open-minded when their children need their help and their direction in making the right choices. And who of all people should our children come to without being afraid? They should come to us, their parents, their friends, the ones who care deeply for them, the ones who love them and desire to instill trust and honesty within them.

Cheryl, it is God's forgiveness and tenderness that heals. It is forgiving ourselves that restores joy and frees us to live with zest and enables us to stop running from both life and death. Peace creates the calm we need to go on with life.

The plot of your book is filled with abundant pain, sorrow, tragedy, doubt, despair, disappointment, and betrayal. Many of the villains are also the heroes, in a sense. A good ending is not always a happy ending. A good ending is one that leads us to believe. A good ending is a seed of faith planted where hope remains.

I was very touched as I read the rough copy of your book. It showed me that I should never prejudge anyone or any situation, because we never know what someone is going through or what he or she is experiencing in their life.

Your music CD entitled "Make Me Your Choice" is a definite WOW!!! I wish you well on the musical play and can't wait to see it.

I hope your efforts touch many lives and enlighten many as they face crucial decisions and that they will find their bright star of hope!

Thank you for letting me see outside my box!

Love,

Stephanie

1

Make Me Your Choice

Have you ever made a choice in life that followed you around constantly and made you ponder, remember, and then ask, "Did I make the right choice?" Sometimes, when we're making our life choices and decisions, we try to take the easy way out, and that gives us quick relief for the moment. However, later on down the road of life the effects of a decision that was not well thought out will cause us a lifetime of pain and remorse.

The conditions of our lives are dependent upon the choices we make. Some choices will have a short-term effect, while other choices will cause us a lifetime of anguish, pain, and heartache. It is amazing how our choices in life will either follow us around like a good dream or become a bad nightmare. Just like a haunting ghost that is constantly hovering over us and reminding us of yesterday's bad choices, the haunting memories of past years prevent us from walking in present and future happiness or joy. Depression and sadness become our way of life.

Our choices in life are never truly private decisions, because what we think and do will always affect many people—those closest to us, those around us, and those of future generations. Our choices in life will help dictate the norms and rules of life for future societies, as well.

In this sense, then, our choices and decisions are very public actions, and they are paramount to the health and direction of society. Our choices—yours, mine, and everyone's—are very important to all of life, for they affect the issues, ethics, standards, morality, and the freedom of choice and life for each member of society.

Throughout the day, into the wee hours of the night, and into the early dawn, someone is crying out. It is a muffled cry that is heard around the world. Approximately every 1.5 seconds, if you listen very carefully, you can hear a muffled cry as a woman, or a woman and a man, are making their choice. Every 1.5 seconds someone is having an abortion somewhere in the world, and a baby's muffled voice is crying out, "Make me your choice!" With every blink of the eye, someone is making a choice.

Sometimes in these cases the choice is made by our own personal decision or by other people who are in control of our lives. Sometimes the choice we make is made out of fear, a mistake, feelings of inconvenience, ignorance, financial difficulties, uncertainty, rape, incest, medical reasons, and the list goes on. The justification for many is that this was the best decision at the time, that there was no other choice. But was it the best decision?

The Bible says, *"There is a way that seems right to a man, but its end is the way of death"* (Prov. 14:12 NKJV).

If you have gone through the hurtful experience of having to make this choice, then I hope with every beat of my heart that this book will help you ease your pain and your anguish. If you are in the process of making a choice, I pray that these heartfelt words will help you make the right choice.

2

God, You Are the Restorer of My Soul

CHERYL'S STORY

It's no mistake that God is fine-tuning my life according to His will, and He still has a lot of perfecting to do in me. But, as I look back upon my life, I must remember that God does not make any mistakes. However, man does. We make mistakes when we fall out of God's perfect will and into the realm of our willful egos. I thank God for His grace, mercy, unconditional love, forgiveness, and what He did for us at Calvary.

It is only through God's redeeming grace—knowing why Jesus died on Calvary, and knowing that His love surrounds me—that I can share my sad story with you. I am able to do this without disgrace or dishonor because His grace is so merciful, plentiful, and beautiful.

Of all the issues and problems I have had to face in my life, none was more prevalent or painful than the issues of sexual purity, sanctity of life, and abortion. Therefore, remaining silent is no longer an option for me. The heartaches and self-condemnation of 21 years that were brought on by wrong choices, irresponsible acts, and personal decisions all need to be faced, dealt with, purified, and cleansed by our Lord's forgiveness, my forgiveness of myself, and the forgiveness I extend to others. And it is only because of God's redeeming grace that I can tell you my story.

Being Asian and having been born into a third-world culture where Buddha was our spiritual leader, I did not get to know Jesus personally until almost 20 years ago. My grandparents were Buddhists. My parents, who were born in America, had no apparent thoughts about religion, and thus they left my brother, sister, and me to seek God and higher truths on our own. However, we were taught to believe that one earns his or her way to Heaven through good works.

They did instill strict moral ethics and traditions in us, however. For example, they taught us that it should be "an eye for an eye, and a tooth for a tooth." They also said that if you choose to sin, you will have to pay for it. In other words, "If you make your bed, you have to lie in it."

The Chinese culture leads us to believe that you shouldn't fear God as much as you fear your parents or those in authority over you. The family is very important in our culture, and any dishonor or disgrace you bring upon your family results in being disowned, whether you are the favorite child or not. And I was the favorite child of my father.

In my senior year of college, I became engaged to my fiance. We were to be married after I graduated from pharmacy school that July. Everything seemed to be coming together so beautifully in my life. It was an exciting time, for wedding bells would soon be ringing, I would be graduating, and a bright and shining future of living happily ever after was about to begin. Or so I thought. Regrettably, I did not see the road-block that was ahead. Something was about to happen that would alter the course of my life and remove the "happily ever after" scenario from my future—I became pregnant in January!

Knowledge of my pregancy brought great fear to me, and panic set in. How could I walk down the aisle on my wedding day while being seven months pregnant? Wedding plans had already been set, and more than 1,000 people had been invited. How could I bring shame and disgrace upon both of our families? The thought of being disowned by my family seemed worse than death. I loved my mother and father very much and to think of being separated from them was unimaginable and unbearable.

After much crying, careful deliberation, and fighting with fear, my fiancé and I chose to have an abortion. It was this sin of abortion, though, that destroyed the love in our marriage. My fiance was a doctor, and I was a pharmacist. We were both in our professions to save lives, and yet we knowingly decided to take a life. Nobody could tell us that there was just "fetal tissue" in me, for we both knew better.

Nonetheless, we scheduled the abortion during my semester break; it would take place at the hospital where my fiancé had completed his internship. He knew the chief of the Ob/gyn Department, and that doctor performed the procedure. In order to have the abortion, though, I had to attend two psychiatric evaluation sessions—to make sure I was making the right decision.

After listening and seeing how distraught and terrified I was, because of the issues surrounding family and parental shame, not to mention the likelihood of being disowned by my parents, the psychiatrist agreed that the abortion should proceed. It was scheduled in the hospital and accomplished in short order.

I returned to school and worked hard to complete my last semester. With finals, graduation, studying for the Pharmacy State Bar Exam, and planning our wedding, there was little time to think of what we had done.

We had a beautiful wedding. It truly was a little girl's dream come true. Next to the birth of our four precious children, it was one of the happiest days of my life. I had my knight in shining armor to love, honor, cherish, and protect me. Or so I thought.

Three weeks after we were married and after the honeymoon was over, my husband stopped kissing me. This hurt me very deeply. Now I can look back upon it, and understand what caused the change in him. Because of the sin we had both committed, my husband simply couldn't face me.

Every time he looked at me, he remembered our sin—our choice. The memory of the abortion tormented him just as much as it did me, but we handled our anguish and torment in different ways. While I felt a need for him to draw closer to me in order to show me that he still loved me, he pushed me away. How differently we reacted to each other! I pray that one day he will also be able to receive Jesus, as I have done, and receive the love, forgiveness, and peace that I now have. In this way he will be able to forgive himself and to forgive me for making and causing him to make that choice.

O dear Father God, I pray for salvation and peace for him. I pray and ask this in the name of Jesus.

Our sexual and love life was completely destroyed. All the love and tenderness were gone, and our relationship became like a mechanical act to us. We just existed, and our marriage, our home, and our hearts were empty. We were like empty shells or empty tombs; we were just going through the routine of life and living. But were we really living? No, we were just existing. In fact, we were like zombies—the living dead—and our lives were very robotic in nature. I constantly felt deep pain and anguish, and I would find myself crying out, "Why, God?"

Three months after our wedding, I felt I had made another mistake by getting married. But, according to our culture, getting a divorce was totally unthinkable. Again, there was the possible shame and disgrace that a divorce would bring to the family. I had made my bed, and I had to lie in it; in other words, I had to face the music that my choices had created.

The people we knew thought we were living in a fairy-tale world. As our marriage went on, we became the parents of four beautiful children. I always appeared to be the happy, obedient wife, and my husband was always the good provider. The Chinese culture dictates that you shouldn't let anyone see your heart or your pain; you must bear it alone and keep it to yourself, all the while showing the world a happy and smiling face. If you have grief or sorrow, you simply must bear it. You just keep on smiling to the world and saying, "Everything is good, beautiful, and fine here." You are expected to do these things even if your heart is breaking and death is at your door.

The first ten years of our marriage were busy years of child-bearing and child-raising. I was helping my husband get his medical practice established during those years. We were so busy that we didn't give much thought to the bondage of sin we were under. We just kept ourselves so busy and tired that our thoughts and feelings were numbed.

As our marriage continued into its eighth year, my husband's father and his best friend died, causing him to slip into a deeper depression. In the aftermath, our relationship deteriorated further.

It was also during this time that my husband began to tell me that I wasn't good enough, and that I didn't deserve anything nice. There were times when he wouldn't speak to me for weeks or months on end, even though I was the one who was managing his office practice. I had given up my career as a pharmacist to help him in his medical practice. Any questions that I needed him to answer would be answered with either a "yes" or "no." Other than that, there were no other discussions, communication, or physical contact. Our relationship consisted of icy silence and isolation.

How my heart grieved and ached during those years. I loved this man unconditionally. I did everything I could to try to please him and to get him to love me. Indeed, I gave him all of me, all that I had. However, he couldn't give me any part of himself, for he was so tied up by the bondage of anger and unforgiveness that had stemmed from our sin.

I began to believe that I was unworthy, and I became crippled with my own thoughts of unworthiness due to our sin. I felt absolutely worthless and valueless, and I began to think, "Why am I here? Will I ever feel love and tenderness again? Will I ever be cherished, treasured, or loved again?"

For 12 years I stayed in an emotionally abusive and starved relationship until it almost became the death of me. It seemed as if no one really cared or loved me except for my four precious little children who loved me so unconditionally. I thanked God for sending them to me. It was their love that sustained me, and they gave me the reason to keep on living.

Because we were not going to church during those years, we fell into the New Age teaching of the "Me" generation through which one would intellectualize, rationalize, psychologize, and "philosophize" about everything. This gave us various "answers" to life, but they would not point us in the correct way or give us the right answer for our lives. These approaches brought us no true peace, and they gave us no final resolution to our dilemma.

People think that having an abortion is a quick fix, a mend-all for an accident or a bad mistake. Some will reason that nobody will know about it, and nobody will see the awful thing we did and what sinful people we are. Let me tell you, this is a lie straight from the devil's pit. Abortion *does* hurt. It always carries severe consequences with it. Abortion not only kills the little baby, but it affects and even destroys all life around it. I know, for it destroyed my marriage and relationship with my family and relatives and put me under a bondage of unworthiness, depression, guilt, shame, and self-condemnation for more than 20 years.

For more than two decades I felt very unworthy. How could God love and forgive such a horrible person as me—a person who took the life of another person, my very own baby? With these self-defeating thoughts constantly in my mind, the imprisonment of my mind and soul became my living hell. I tried to lead a good and righteous life, and I prayed to God for forgiveness of my sins. Yet, in my mind and heart, I thought, "How could God ever forgive me for destroying a life?" I believed I was going straight to hell. I knew and believed I couldn't do enough good works here on earth to earn the privilege to even touch the steps of Heaven because of my sins.

I began psychotherapy with a woman therapist, and she helped me find the strength to leave my sad marriage. She told me that we all deserve love, tenderness, respect, honor, and communication in our relationships; because this is what God has ordained in matrimony for all of His children, and it is the devil who wants to rob us of that. She told me that I was a beautiful, accomplished, and worthy lady, and she helped me to look at myself differently.

As time went on, I began to realize that I was good (at heart???), and that I was an accomplished and worthy lady. When I started attending counseling sessions, however, I was a true "basket case." I felt so worthless due to how my husband treated me, what he said to me, and my awareness of my own sin. I felt ugly.

I was in a deep depression, and found myself crying many times each day and night. You could have scraped me off the bottom of your shoe like a wad of old, spit-out, used-up chewing gum. This was my life, and this was how I felt about myself. Without realizing it, I had based my entire sense of self-esteem on the words and actions of my husband. I felt valueless.

It was difficult for me to talk to my parents about my family situation, for they lived 600 miles away, and I did not want to burden them with my problems and have them worry about my unhappiness and the four children. I felt they wouldn't have understood, anyway. So after my husband and I separated, it took me two months to finally get enough courage to tell my parents about it. It upset my father so much that for six months he could not and would not speak to me whenever I called home.

With His Help

It was then that I started reaching out to God. I prayed and asked Him if He would help me with my situation. I asked Him to give me strength and courage to endure and change.

During this time, God placed His hand upon my life in a very profound way. He provided me with a new vocation. Although I had been a mother, pharmacist, office manager, and handler of all the finances in our marriage, God led me to become a jeweler who dealt with fine jewelry even while I was managing my husband's office. I manufactured and designed beautiful gold and diamond jewelry. As a result of my new career direction, my self-esteem and self-worth began to grow, and my new-found business also started to grow and prosper.

When we are not right with God we start walking in the flesh. Out of loneliness and despair, we turn to human beings for the satisfaction of our needs and to find our own personal happiness and sense of security. We always fall when we are functioning in the flesh. Three and a half years after I was separated from my husband, I fell into an adulterous relationship with a married man, and, as a result, I became pregnant.

This time I went to my prayer closet and cried out, "Oh, my God, it's the same lesson as before! Please help me!" I was 36 years old and had four kids. I was barely making ends meet and I owed the Internal Revenue

Service $50,000 in income taxes incurred during our marriage. My husband and I shared in our community assets, but we also shared in our community debts. What was I to do?

In the flesh I began to think, "How could I have another child?" Again, a deep sense of shame and embarrassment overwhelmed me. I really did not want to marry the man I was involved with, for that would require the destruction of his marriage. Then there was the realization that the sin of abortion could be imminent. I was fearful of so many things again. Nonetheless, I chose to have an abortion, and I ended my adulterous affair. Once again the issues of sexual purity, sanctity of life, and abortion haunted me; and now the added sin of adultery pressed in on me.

For the next two years, I became even more of a workaholic. I threw all of my energies into my business and my children while pulling the weight of my sins behind me. I turned to alcohol to ease the pain and torment I felt.

In the evenings after the kids went to bed and the lights were turned low, the reality of my troubled life overwhelmed me. Alcohol helped me sleep and numb my troubling thoughts and pain. However, when I awoke each morning, the tormenting thoughts would still be there.

The pain of sin is always so difficult to bear. I thought if I worked harder and spent longer hours working and tried to live a more righteous life, that people would not see or know of my sins, and I could hide in my prayer closet. It was right after the adulterous affair that I realized that adultery is a moral sin, and it hurts all persons connected with it.

While trying to make sense of my life and finding out that men and alcohol were not the solutions to my problems or the key to inner peace or happiness, I discovered the real answer. The answer was always there, but I just hadn't realized it.

The true and only solution to my problems was prayer. So I asked the Lord's forgiveness for my adultery and abortion, and I asked God to come into my life and take over my life completely. I told Him that I would never make those sinful mistakes again. This was the beginning of surrendering my life to God.

When God came into my life, He forgave me instantly, but a long process of deliverance and inner healing was still needed. I thank God each and every day of my life for His mercy and compassion, for His hand upon my life, His redeeming grace, His forgiveness, and His loving patience.

When I surrendered my life to God, He started changing me inside and out. Through prayer He gave me the concept of a new business. God had transformed my jewelry business into a successful woman's boutique and has enabled it to withstand the throes of recession. Just as He guided and changed it from being a flashy, ready-to-wear boutique into a beautiful bridal salon, He guided my spiritual walk and changed me from one who had fallen from grace to one who is the Bride of Christ. He showed me that life takes a lot of hard work, perseverance, steadfastness, forgiveness, obedience, trust in Him, and a total commitment to His Word if we are to be successful in living life to the fullest.

As we line up our lives with Jesus and the Word, we can go forward in faith, victory, love, and peace, and we can persevere with a great sense of purpose. I can now see the purpose and call that are upon my life: to assist the Lord in preparing His Bride (all believers in the Body of Christ) to walk down the aisle of life. I thank God each and every day for His faith and trust in me, for I know He has called me to fulfill His will, even though I am such an unworthy child. It is a privilege and honor to serve Him.

Isn't it wonderful that we serve such a loving God, One who receives us and loves us even when we fail? He is always there for us, waiting for us to fall back into His merciful, loving, forgiving, and restoring hands. When we reach out to receive His grace, we must do so with a truly receptive and repentive heart. We must turn away from all that is not holy or acceptable to God and renew our minds to be like Christ.

Always remember that it is through God that all things are possible. When you start to yield and surrender to God, when you give Him the purity of your heart, your mind, your life, and your love, then He will give you the full blessings of your inheritance in the Kingdom of God, which He wants to give to all of His precious children.

We are all children of God. When you become the Bride of Christ, His very own Bride, He will transform you and make you brand-new, and you will become as white as snow.

Though your sins are like scarlet, they shall be as white as snow (Isaiah 1:18).

He will take you out of darkness, and He will let you walk in victory with Christ. Thank you, Jesus, for your redeeming grace.

I, even I, am he who blots out your transgressions, for my own sake, and remembers your sins no more (Isaiah 43:25).

God took me from being a no one and He raised me up in the community and the church. He fine-tuned, shaped, and molded me. As I yielded to His precious Holy Spirit, He blessed my life. God wants only the best and highest life for all of His children. He tells you wonderful things. He tells you how much He loves you and that you are the apple of His eye. (See Psalm 17:8.) He gives you wonderful ideas.

It's only the devil who wants to rob you of all that God has for you and everything else that's good. The devil will tell you, "You can't do it; you're not good enough; you're not worthy." Those are lies straight from the devil's pit, because everything God created is good. You are good; in fact, you are very good! Moreover, you are created in the image and likeness of God, and you can do all things through Christ who will strengthen and develop you. (See Philippians 4:13.)

With God, there is no limit. Nothing is impossible with God. I thank God for loving me so much and not placing any limits on my talents and abilities. He wants us to achieve our highest potential. This can only occur once we start to yield, surrender, and listen to Him in complete obedience and faith.

This should be our prayer: Dear heavenly Father, I want whatever is Your perfect will. Let Your will not mine be done. Mold me and shape me into all that you want me to be. Let your Holy Spirit flow through me to guide me, strengthen me, and fill me. Direct me to all that you want me to be for your glory and for your service, dear Lord in Jesus' name. Amen.

And, yes, that is why I love God so much. He took me out of darkness, made me white as snow, and I became His bride, the Bride of Christ. He healed my pain and my soul, and He took away the agony, torment, and unhappiness of my life. He raised me up in the community and took me out of debt. He gave me riches way beyond everything I ever thought or imagined I could ever achieve or deserve.

At the Cross—From Our Crossroad to Our Call

Since the time of my deliverance, the Lord has been asking me to step out and tell my story and venture forth into ministry. I asked, "Father, how can you expect such an unworthy vessel as me to speak the Word of God?"

He said, "*Child, I love you.*"

I protested, "But, Father, the abortions. How could you love and forgive such a horrible person as me?"

He said, "*My child, look back upon your life. If I hadn't forgiven you for the abortions, would I have blessed you with your four beautiful children?*"

I thought about it and replied, "That's right, if you were a vengeful God, you would have taken away my right to childbearing."

He tenderly answered, "*That's right, I loved you so much that I blessed you with the desires of your heart. Remember when you were engaged and you told everyone how you wanted five children? I gave you five, and because I heard your prayers that first time, you now have four beautiful and wonderful children. I understood why you made the choice of abortion because you feared being disowned and thought you had no other choice. I heard your prayers for forgiveness and I knew you were remorseful.*"

I stammered, "But, Father, what about the second abortion and the adultery, how could you have forgiven me of those sins?"

The Lord replied, "*Did I not bless you with the concept of Allusions, a new business that would always be blessed? I heard your cry of repentance, your prayer of forgiveness, and your promise that you would turn away from your sins, which you did. I forgave you then again, My child.*"

With great sobs I replied, "O my God, yes you did!"

Then God showed me a vision of Jesus on the cross. I will never forget that vision. It was so vivid and horrific that it is forever burned into my mind's memory.

He asked, "*Why do you think I died on Calvary for you? Why do you think My blood was shed? With the nailing of My hand upon the cross, that first abortion was forgiven, and with the nailing of My other hand, the second abortion was forgiven. With the nailing of My feet, I took away that sin of adultery. With the piercing of My rib, I took away the sin of alcoholism. With every lash of the whip that I took upon My body, I took away all of your other sins. With the wreath of thorns that was crushed upon My head I am now taking away your torment, anguish, shame, guilt and pain. My child, I loved you so much that I died for you and forgave you.*"

I cried, "O my God, all these years you forgave me and loved me and you have been waiting for me to forgive myself."

He tenderly replied, "*Yes, that is right, My child, I forgave you the minute you prayed it. I have been waiting all these years for you to forgive yourself. Twenty-one years of guilt, shame, self-condemnation, and anguish is much too long for any of My children to have to endure. Even one year, one month, one week, or even one day is too much for My children to endure. How it grieved My heart to watch you crying night after night. I wanted to hold you in My arms to let you know how much I loved you and that you were forgiven, but you didn't invite Me into your heart or life. You only asked for forgiveness, and I immediately forgave you. I could only stand silently behind you, watching sadly over you. I want all of My children to know that the minute they get on their knees and say, 'Abba, Father, please forgive me of all of my sin; I give you my life, my heart, my mind, and my spirit,' I forgive them at that precise moment.*"

Remember, God will forgive you if you ask and if you invite Him into your heart and life. He will change you and make you brand new, and you will walk in His redeeming grace and go from glory to glory to glory with the Lord.

> "*Praise the Lord, O my soul, and forget not all his benefits—who forgives all your sins and heals all your diseases, who redeems your life from the pit and crowns you with love and compassion, who satisfies your desires with good things so that your youth is renewed like the eagle's*" (Ps. 103:2-5).

Then God asked me, "*Cheryl, will you tell your story and share My love and forgiveness with others?*"

Sadly, I replied, "Lord, I can't. The church and the people—they are so critical. They will persecute and judge me and they will look down upon me. I am sorry, I just can't." I was so afraid of what other people would think about me, that they wouldn't like me, and that they would shun me once they knew about what I'd done.

Then God showed me a huge inferno that was ablaze with fire everywhere. There were thousands upon thousands of faceless souls being consumed by the fire. Then He said, "*Are you going to let all these people perish in hell because you refuse to tell them of My love and forgiveness?*"

As I protested that I couldn't, He asked why not. I replied, "Because of my business in the community, my position in the church, and even the fact that I have been on Christian TV!"

God answered, "*Who do you think put you in those places? Just as fast as I raised you up, I can bring you down.*"

I protested fearfully, "But God, the people are going to crucify me because of what I did, they will shun and condemn me."

Then God said, "*Cheryl, did I condemn you? Did I forsake you? Just remember, you used to be one of those faceless people in the inferno! Now, will you tell the people of My love, My goodness, and My redeeming grace, and tell them about the plan and purpose I have for their lives?*"

And then God flashed the vision of the fiery inferno in front of me again and said, "*You once were there!*"

I tearfully replied, "Yes, God! I will tell them all about You and how wonderful You are."

So God wants all who have suffered from abortion and its pain to know that He loves them. He loves you so very, very much, and He wants to forgive you. Therefore, be sure to renounce all of your sins and transgressions and come before the Lord. Go to the throne of God, and cast out all of your vast imaginations and spirits of unworthiness, depression, despair, helplessness, anger, self-anger, hatred, self-condemnation, self-denial, self-hatred, and the spirit of rationalism and intellectualism, along with the spirit of error and death.

The Lord Jesus stands beside you right now, and He will replace all those ill feelings and strongholds with His great mercy and redeeming grace, and He will fill you with His perfect love and His Holy Spirit.

So, today, if you would like to achieve a closer relationship with God, He is with you right now. Please receive Jesus as your Lord and Savior. I can assure you that your life will never be the same once you touch the hem of His garment.

> *When you were dead in your sins and in the uncircumcision of your sinful nature, God made you alive with Christ. He forgave us all our sins, having canceled the written code, with its regulations, that was against us and that stood opposed to us; he took it away, nailing it to the cross. And having disarmed the powers and authorities, he made a public spectacle of them, triumphing over them by the cross* (Colossians 2:13-15).

> *And suddenly, a woman who had a flow of blood for twelve years came from behind and touched the hem of His garment. For she said to herself, "If only I may touch His garment, I shall be made well." But Jesus turned around, and when He saw her He said, "Be of good cheer daughter, your faith has made you well." And the woman was made well from that hour* (Matthew 9:20-22 NKJV).

Pray as follows: Dear Lord, I repent of all of my sins. Please forgive me of all of my sins. I thank you for Jesus who died on the cross for all of my sins so that I can come back into right relationship with you. I receive Jesus into my life now as my Lord and Savior. In Jesus' name I pray, Amen.

> *That if you confess with your mouth, "Jesus is Lord," and believe in your heart that God raised him from the dead, you will be saved. For it is with your heart that you believe and are justified, and it is with your mouth that you confess and are saved. As the Scripture says, "Anyone who trusts in Him will never be put to shame"* (Romans 10:9-11).

Our life story consists of our life choices. How we choose to succeed over our bad choices or succumb to their negative consequences will be our test in life. Our testing will be our testimony that will tell of our initial failure and then our subsequent victory to overcome any situation. Will God be part of your victory and your testimony?

3

Thank You, Dear Friend

I can never thank Laurie Crouch enough for her love and friendship. Seventeen years ago, unbeknownst to her, she ministered to me, and did so many other times too numerous to mention. I specifically remember a time when Laurie was over at my house for lunch. She was sad and depressed because she had recently miscarried her second child.

As I was preparing lunch for us in the kitchen, Laurie begin to share with me what a beautiful friend had shared with her in her Bible study group. This friend had said, "Laurie, don't be sad. Your babies were so perfect that God took them directly up to Heaven to minister to all the aborted babies in Heaven."

When I heard that, my heart jumped for joy, because I had been agonizing and wondering, "Whatever happened to my two aborted babies? Where are they now?" Now I knew where they were; my two precious babies were up in Heaven being ministered to and loved by Laurie's two babies. I wanted to hug Laurie and tell her how thankful I was for what she told me. But, because I was so locked up in my secret sins, experiencing shame and guilt and fearing condemnation from people, I remained silent.

Finally, I said, "Laurie, that is so beautiful and wonderful for all the aborted babies." On that very day, God used Laurie to help unlock the prison door of my self-imprisonment, but because of the anguish and unforgiveness that I held against myself, I continued to sit silently in my self-locked cell.

It was not long after lunch that day when God showed me the vision of the inferno that I recounted in the preceding chapter. It was then that I told God, "OK, I will share my testimony and story." If I was going to be persecuted by the church, I might as well find out about it now.

I called my dear friend, "Hi, Laurie. How are you?"

Cheerfully she replied, "I'm fine, Cheryl. What's up?"

Hesitantly I said, "I just wanted to share something with you."

"What is it?"

Meekly I responded, "Laurie, before I got married, I had an abortion with my husband."

As Laurie spoke, her voice got very soft and she tenderly responded, "Oh, Cheryl, my heart goes out to you. You know the people in the church need to reach out and help the people going through the pains of abortion. They need to help them overcome the anguish, pain, and guilt instead of imposing judgment on them. How can I help you?"

Because of the thoughts of my own self-condemnation and shame at the time, I couldn't share with Laurie about the second abortion. It was hard enough telling her about the first one. I felt that telling about the first one was enough, possibly too much for anyone to understand anyway.

It was Laurie's compassion, love, and non-judgementalism that brought about my total deliverance from shame, self-condemnation, guilt, and fear of other people and their thoughts and judgments. That day I walked out of my self-imposed jail cell and started to live life fully, with a new and wonderful sense of joy. I was free at last!

Laurie truly walks in the steps of Jesus, showing and sharing His Love and compassion to all who comes in contact with her.

Thank you, my dear friend, for your hand of friendship, love, and understanding.

> *If one falls down, his friend can help him up. But pity the man who falls and has no one to help him up!"* (Ecclesiastes 4:10)

> *Dear friends, since God so loved us, we also ought to love one another* (1 John 4:11).

> *There is no fear in love. But perfect love drives out fear* (1 John 4:18).

> *Perfume and incense bring joy to the heart, and the pleasantness of one's friend springs from his earnest counsel* (Proverbs 27:9).

4

And the Beat Goes On

LORNAH'S STORY

I have known my friend, Lornah, for over 15 years. When I mentioned to her that I was writing this book, she told me she had a story to tell and proceeded to share her story with me. Remaining silent was no longer an option for her either. As Lornah shares her heart in the following paragraphs, may her testimony bring peace and resolution to your life or to the life of a loved one.

This is Lornah's story.

Our secret sins have a way of following us through the next generations. While dating my father, my mother became pregnant and my dad convinced her to have an abortion. Later, pregnant again with my sister, they decided to keep her and got married. Two years after the birth of my sister, my mother became pregnant again, this time with me.

My father tried to persuade her to abort me, saying that he was convinced that the child she was carrying was not his. This was not true, but, because she feared my father, she made the secretive arrangements and went to the doctor. Much to her surprise, Dr. Smith told her to go home, for he would not perform the procedure she asked for. Frightened, she went home to "pay the price" for her disobedience. Dad then left for a few days to get drunk and to find another woman to console him!

My alcoholic father barely tolerated me. As I was growing up, he would beat me during his frequent drunken rages. To him, I was a constant reminder of everything he didn't want.

At age 16, after a very severe beating, I ran away. I called my boyfriend and begged him to take me away. I never wanted to return home again. I thought my hopes were realized when my boyfriend promised to take care of me. The night he agreed to do so was a night that would change my life and would forever be etched in my memory. That night my boyfriend, JC, took my virginity against my will.

My hopes were shattered when he brought me back home in the wee hours of the morning and broke up with me. There I was, having been beaten by my father and raped and rejected by the friend I thought I could trust. I was completely devastated. Deep down, I thought there must be something very wrong with me that both the men in my life didn't want me. What had I done to cause this?

As time went on and I missed my period, I panicked. This would prove that my dad was right when he said, "You are no good, and you are nothing but a problem for mom and me!" I had no money or job, no car to take me to the doctor, and, being 16, I felt I had no other option but to try and abort the baby myself.

Therefore, I took castor oil and "quinine" tablets and sat in a hot bathtub hour after hour while my parents were away. I also went horseback riding, and I tried inserting a coat hanger into my vagina in order to abort the baby myself, but all of this was to no avail. I was greatly tormented in my thinking. Fear would overcome and consume me throughout the late night hours, as I would cry myself to sleep each night.

In anguish I wondered, "What am I going to do?" I remember thinking that if there was a God, He sure didn't know that I existed, but, at the same time, I felt I didn't deserve a break after what I had done. (As I look back upon it now, the God I didn't yet know was protecting my beautiful baby girl who would soon become the richest blessing of my life.)

As the months passed, I could no longer hide my growing tummy. I finally went to my mother with the news of my pregnancy and told her I was about four months along. In a panic, she told me that this would mar her reputation as an elementary school principal who was well-known in the educational community. She went on to say, "What would they think of me having a daughter like you? How could you do this to me? And what about your father? This proves he was right about you being no good. How can we stop him from doing what he might do to us when he finds out?"

She took me immediately to a doctor and asked for an abortion, as there was no way she would let me keep the baby. Dr. Jones told us that I was too far along and that he would not perform the abortion. However, he would deliver the baby for free and would like to have his good friends adopt the baby. He looked at me with eyes of mercy and love, and I felt no condemnation from him. In fact, his tenderness and acceptance made me cry. I had never seen such compassion in a man before. The doctor and my mother made all the arrangements for me, and we went home to wait for the baby's arrival.

Mom came up with a plan to conceal it all from my father. Mom and dad were having marital problems, and he was ready to move out anyway. So, she would just get him to move out sooner and then we wouldn't have to pay for his rage.

The plan was not to tell anyone about my pregnancy; it would be a secret between my mother and me. Not even my older married sister was to know. My mother planned to tell the school officials that I had developed a serious kidney disease and had to remain on bed rest. After all, they would most likely believe another principal.

I never left the house. I stayed there each day by myself. It was like being in a prison, and I never felt more alone than I did during that time, locked up in the consequences of my predicament. I hated myself for causing this. When anyone would come over, I would quickly jump into bed in order to hide my stomach. This went on for a several months until one day, my sister and her husband dropped by in the morning after my mother had left for work. I didn't have time to get in bed, so I ran into a closet to hide. I was seven months pregnant at the time. I sat in the dark hoping they would leave soon, but instead they stayed all day. The weight of the child on my organs made me have to go to the bathroom. I could no longer hold it. Therefore, I had to sit all day in my own excrement, as I silently cried, wishing that I had never been born. By the time mom got home and they left, it was evident that I could not go on like this.

Mom told everyone that she was taking me away to get help for my kidney disease. Mother placed me in a Catholic home for unwed mothers. There, I had to work in the laundry room washing and drying hospital bedding. I was unable to sit down for prolonged periods in the intense heat, and then I was told that I needed to deliver this baby with no anesthetic in order to atone for my sins. Eventually, I collapsed and fell into a deep, dark depression. A kind nun came to my rescue and called my mother after she recognized the frailty and vulnerability of my mental and emotional state.

Mom came and got me. Now what was she going to do with me? We checked into a motel a few miles away. I took walks while she was at work, hoping to prompt the birth to come early. I just wanted to get it over with. Once, while I was walking, the father of my child passed by in his car. I could see that he had his arm around a girl who was sitting very close to him. My heart sank, and I couldn't stop crying.

At the doctor's suggestion, we went in to have the baby induced early. I awoke with a flat tummy. They wouldn't let me see the baby, for they knew that would be too hard on me with regard to making the decision to give her up. Adoption papers were brought in, but somehow, I couldn't bring myself to sign them. The couple who wanted my baby took her home with them.

We went home. I had been "cured" of my "kidney disease," and life at age 17 was to begin again. Three months later, I could no longer contain the longing I felt for my child. I kept trying to ignore those haunting, torment-ing emotions that kept rising to the surface. I couldn't think of anything else. All I knew was that I wanted my baby. Against my mother's threats, I left to find her. When mom saw that I meant it and had left home, she called the doctor and arranged for us to go and get my baby back.

It was excruciatingly painful for the couple that had my daughter to give her up. I hurt for them as much or perhaps even more than I did for me. Sadly, they gave my baby back to me, and we took her home. Suddenly, there she was in my arms—a beautiful baby girl with locks of reddish hair. Tears flowed from my eyes as I looked at her. My heart melted and then it pounded with excitement, love, and fear. We had no diapers, food, or necessities. I was still in high school, and I had no source of income. Now what?

Mom came up with another plan. Still, no one was to know that the baby belonged to me, because that would bring disgrace upon my mother. How could I ruin her career? The guilt I carried for causing all of these problems was already unbearable. My mother proceeded to call my sister and told her that a mother at her school was dying and needed someone to help take care of her baby, and that she would be paid for doing it. My sister agreed, for she needed extra money. Mom was willing to pay almost anything to keep this covered up.

I would visit my sister once a week, or as often as someone would take me to her home. She was very protective of the baby, and many times she would not let me feed or hold her. Inside, I felt like a little part of me was slowly dying. It was so hard to walk away with all these secrets inside of me. When would I become a true mother to my child? I convinced myself that maybe I wasn't a good-enough mother anyway and that she was better off with my sister.

Many months passed until one day baby Heidi was rushed to the hospital with a serious infection, and she had to be quarantined. All of my family (sister, mother, father, and his new wife) gathered outside her hospital room, permitted only to peek through the door window.

My sister was distraught because her husband thought it was now time to give the baby back to her real mother. I could not continue with the lies any longer. I took a deep breath and blurted out, "You don't have to give Heidi back, because she's *my* baby, and I am taking her home with me. She belongs to *me!*" My mother gasped out loud, and she looked like someone had just stung her with a laser gun. My father put his head down and turned pale.

At first, my sister rebuked me for such a tasteless joke. I went on to explain everything, right there in front of everybody, nurses and all. I was proud to announce that Heidi was my baby. As the tears began to flood her eyes, my sister grabbed me and said, "Why didn't you tell me? I could have been there for you throughout your pregnancy."

My father quietly paid the hospital bill and never said another word about it.

I brought *my* Heidi home when she got well and now everyone knew she was mine. My sister continued to babysit for her until I graduated from high school and was able to get a job and find my own apartment. Life as a single mom was not easy. I did a lot of things correctly, but I also made many mistakes along the way.

As a young mother, I made some poor choices in my struggles to raise my daughter. Loneliness drove me to look for love in all the wrong places. I didn't know then what I do know now—God is the answer for my emptiness. Still trying to put my life together by myself, I married a man who had traits similar to my father.

A couple of years after my marriage, I became pregnant again. My excitement soon turned to resignation as my husband advocated for an abortion and tried to convince me that another child would take much away from our lives. I asked my Ob/gyn doctor for advice. He not only agreed with my husband, but also led me to believe that I would be responsible for the break-up of my marriage if I did not go through with the abortion.

In light of all this, we went ahead with the abortion. In those days, I felt no guilt, just sadness. I saw this as simply getting rid of a potential problem. It was not long after that I discovered my husband was having an extramarital affair (again), and our marriage ended. Then I understood why he wouldn't let me keep our baby.

The good that came through this was that I found the love of Jesus Christ. I finally turned to God to help make my life right, and my life changed drastically. Becoming secure in His love, I began a great adventure that has brought great meaning and purpose to my life. Knowing that Jesus died to pay for my sins, I asked the Lord to forgive me for having an abortion.

Even so, I still saw the abortion as just the elimination of a fetus rather than taking a life. Thinking that all was well regarding this, I went merrily on my way until a couple of years later. While I was at a baby shower, I suddenly burst into tears. I didn't knowing why I was crying or what was happening to me; I quickly left to find a quiet spot where I could be alone.

As I was asking God to show me what this meant, I suddenly heard a voice saying, "Mommy, I forgive you." Instantly, I knew God was showing me that my baby was with Him, that the baby was not just a fetus, but a child who had been prevented from growing up and fulfilling his/her destiny. Now I knew that I had taken a life and that this act would affect generations to come.

God was not condemning me. He wanted to set me free through a complete healing that involved Him forgiving me and cleansing me totally, not partially. I had asked for forgiveness for a little part of the sin, for destroying a fetus, but I had not recognized the full truth—I had stopped a life that was meant to be lived. God could only forgive that which I had confessed to Him, and He wanted to forgive me of all my sins and set me free from any and all sorrow and condemnation. I began to weep as I realized the full reality of His amazing love. Instantaneously, I felt more love from God than I could possibly process.

I asked for His forgiveness again as I now took responsibility for the truth. As I did so, His love, mercy, and forgiveness overwhelmed me. I walked away totally healed and more in love with the Lord than ever before. We read in the Bible how God forgave David for committing adultery and taking the life of Uriah the Hittite. As soon as David recognized the fullness of his sin, God restored him. On that same night, God gave him the gift of conceiving his son Solomon.

David responded with the following beautiful prayer:

> *Have mercy on me, O God, according to your unfailing love; according to your great compassion blot out my transgressions. Wash away all my iniquity and cleanse me from my sin. For I know my transgressions, and my sin is always before me. . . . Surely you desire truth in the inner parts; you teach me wisdom in the inmost place. Cleanse me with hyssop and I will be clean; wash me, and I will be whiter than snow. . . . Create in me a pure heart, O God, and renew a steadfast spirit within me. . . . Then I will teach*

transgressors your ways, and sinners will turn back to you (Psalm 51:1-3; 6-7;10;13).

Having walked with the Lord now for many years, I am not the same person that I was years ago. I think differently, I react differently, and I am truly different. My life is rich and full, and each day is a new opportunity to rejoice, to enjoy the journey, and to fall more in love with Jesus.

My beautiful daughter, my only child, and I are very close, and we spend very sweet times together. Several years ago, she shared with me the secret she had carried in her heart—when she was a young woman, her boyfriend talked her into having an abortion. Immediately I knew the hurt, shame, and guilt that she had been carrying.

As I told her my story, we cried and forgave each other, recognizing that in the same way God forgave us, we also need to forgive ourselves. We now believe that this generational chain has been broken in our family line and will not be passed down any longer to others.

Today, my daughter is a medical doctor who is happily married, and she and her husband have given me three beautiful grandchildren. Had she been aborted, her children would not have been born, and that family line would have been broken. Additionally, I would never have had or known my greatest treasures here on earth—my precious family. The lives she has helped and saved as a doctor might have been lost, as well. I cherish each moment I have with my family, and I never cease to thank God for them—the richest of all my blessings.

Love,

LORNAH STUMP
Founder of "Woman of Influence"

5

There Is a Loving and Forgiving God

LARRY'S STORY

I met Larry through my business. He was a sales representative for a bridal manufacturer. Larry had a morning appointment with me in my bridal salon; he was going to show me his company's new line for fall. As he came strolling in pushing his rolling rack of bridal gowns, he was humming along with the Christian praise music playing in the background.

He went to the back of the store, where he waited. It caught me by surprise that Larry knew the music, for he was humming all the melodies out loud as if he knew the songs by heart. I thought Larry was a very worldly gentleman who didn't go to church.

After I finished with a customer, I went over to him, and he began to show me his new fall collection. While I was evaluating his bridal line, he continued to hum along with the music. Then we started to talk.

"Larry, I didn't know you were Christian."

He laughingly replied, "I'm not; I'm Jewish."

"But you seem to know the music so well, and you are harmonizing so beautifully with the songs."

He replied, "Oh, I'm a musician, and when I hear music, I just naturally hum or sing along."

Then he asked, "Cheryl, why do you play Christian music in your store? It is so unusual to hear this type of music being played in a store located in a large regional mall."

I explained, "The reason I play Christian music in my store is because it brings me great peace and strength. I play it in thanksgiving to Jesus who loved me and forgave me of all of my sin."

His eyes opened wide as I begin to share the sad story of my abortions with him. At the time, I couldn't understand why I was telling all of this to Larry. I didn't know him that well, and it seemed odd that I would share such intimate information about myself with him. After all, I was just starting to "come out of the closet" by sharing my testimony with people I knew.

When I finished, Larry looked sadly into my eyes and shared with me that he had gone through five abortions—two abortions with two different ladies whom he had been dating and three of them were with his wife.

The first abortion occurred before they got married, and the other two took place during the course of their marriage. Sadly, he couldn't understand why his wife didn't want to keep any of the two babies she had conceived while they were married. He was tormented, angered, and in daily anguish because of the tragic decisions.

Guilt and anger filled their lives. In order to escape the rage and bitterness that was present in their marriage, they increased their abuse of drugs and alcohol. Larry told me that soon after the last abortion, their marriage totally collapsed.

As a result, his family was gone and his life was now in shambles. Larry was brokenhearted and depressed. For most of his adult life, he had been searching for love, resolution, and peace concerning his choices and their entailing consequences. Larry was searching in all the wrong places to solve his problems, and the alcohol and drugs only darkened and deadened him to the pain he was experiencing. Slowly and unwittingly, he was self-destructing and wasting away.

As I looked into his sad brown eyes, I noticed tears of remorse beginning to well up. I softly asked, "Larry, would you like to have the peace I have right now? And would you like to be forgiven of all of your sins?"

He responded quickly by shouting, "Yes!"

I replied, "Then you need to invite Jesus into your life as your Lord and Savior and ask Him to forgive you of all of your sins."

That day Larry received Jesus, and, as he asked Jesus to forgive him and fill him with His love and the precious Holy Spirit, the awesome presence of God filled him.

For a while Larry was immobilized in a state of great peace and love; it was a state of being and feeling that he had never experienced in his life before. In fact, he was so overwhelmed by what he was experiencing that he said he had never felt such great peace come over him along with continuous waves of love. He said, "This felt better than any high I have ever experienced through drugs, sex, or alcohol. What is happening to me?"

I was happy to explain to him that God was filling him with His pure love, great peace, and total forgiveness. At that moment Larry's life was changed forever; that is the awesome power and love of God's redeeming grace.

> *The Lord is close to the brokenhearted and saves those who are crushed in spirit* (Psalm 34:18).

> *He heals the brokenhearted and binds up their wounds* (Psalm 147:3).

> *When I kept silent, my bones wasted away through my groaning all day long. For day and night your hand was heavy upon me; my strength was sapped as in the heat of summer. Then I acknowledged my sin to you and did not cover up my iniquity. I said "I will confess my transgression to the Lord"— and you forgave the guilt of my sin* (Psalm 32:3-5).

> *Ask and it will be given to you; seek and you will find; knock and the door will be opened to you. For everyone who asks receives; he who seeks finds; and to him who knocks, the door will be opened* (Matthew 7:7-8).

> *Everyone who calls on the name of the Lord will be saved* (Romans 10:13).

6

Thou Shalt Not Kill: Exodus 20:13

JIM'S STORY

In the paragraphs that follow Jim shares his story with us:

I have been attending church now for over 12 years and I still continuously carry the pain, regret, and self-condemnation for the choice I inflicted upon my childhood sweetheart 25 years ago, which later caused us to "split up."

Since that day, the choice I made—the one I forced her to make because I was so scared and confused—has haunted me without end. There is not one day that goes by when I do not recall the black Wednesday that changed our lives—the day I took her to the abortion clinic. I hate Wednesdays!

She tried to be so brave and understanding with regard to the burden this child would bring upon us in light of the fact that my new career as a musician was starting to hit. You see, I was getting bookings from clubs up and down the state. How could my career take off with a brand-new baby and wife? I barely had enough money to pay my own traveling expenses to the different gigs. I just couldn't afford the extra cost of having a family. Little did I know how much our decision was going to cost me in the future. I would lose my sweetheart, my soul, and finally my peace of mind.

Our relationship lasted another two years after the abortion, but it kept going steadily downhill. My wife eventually became very depressed. We fought all the time. I was gone very frequently, and she drank excessively to deal with the pain and anger she felt. I couldn't stand the constant fighting, crying, and accusations that she would hurl at me. So I left.

I was very sad as I packed my bags for the last time on a Wednesday night and never returned. The bitterness between us could not be repaired. I hate Wednesdays. To this day, when Wednesdays come I feel dark and empty inside. And so alone.

I know that Jesus has forgiven me, but it still is very hard for me to forgive myself. I made a choice, a decision that literally destroyed my hopes and dreams as a young man. The zeal I once had for life was replaced with an ache in my heart that just won't go away.

Do I deserve love? Do I deserve a family? Do I deserve happiness? I'm still searching, and I'm still trying to put the pieces together and work things out in my head. Relationships have become hard for me. I just can't seem to relate to any woman. It's as if I have this big hole in my heart and no one can fill the void. I've dated some very nice ladies, but nothing ever came of those attempts to build a relationship. The fault wasn't theirs; it was mine. So here I am, sitting all alone day after day, month after month, year after year.

As I sit quietly in the back of the church, my outer demeanor is one of servitude, for I am grateful for the forgiveness I was given for my grave sin. On the outside I offer good works toward others, steadfast faithfulness, and an ever-smiling face, but inside my heart, my soul cries out nightly, weeping for my lost baby and the poor choice that I made. So I sit silently, masked in solitude, in my anguish, as all those tormenting thoughts invade my mind. God, please help me!

In many instances, we only have one chance in this life to make the right decision between two options. If we choose the right path, our decision is a good one. If not, we have to live out the effects that our bad choice created.

Sometimes when I look at children, I feel deeply saddened by what I did. But that was the choice I thought I had to make. It was what I thought was best for me. I was so young and selfish at the time. I didn't know any better. I was only thinking about myself. Everything was so confusing, so heavy on me. It makes me sad to think about it, even more so while I'm sharing this with you.

Now when I think about the baby, I can only pray that other couples will make the right decision. Killing is a sin. Think about it. Maybe we should have given up the child for adoption, or perhaps we should have kept our child. I just don't know. I asked God to forgive me for what I've done. Yes, I still do feel remorse and tremendous guilt for having gone through with the abortion. Even though I know that God has forgiven me, I still beat myself up for it. I do know that God loves us unconditionally and forgives us if we confess our sins to Him. I know He watches over us until the end of time.

My prayer for you is that you will make the right choice. To choose life is to live. To choose abortion is to choose death.

Blessed are those who mourn, for they will be comforted (Matthew 5:4).

. . . God will wipe away every tear from their eyes (Revelation 7:17).

Come to me, all you who are weary and burdened, and I will give you rest. Take my yoke upon you and learn from me, for I am gentle and humble in heart, and you will find rest for your souls. For my yoke is easy and my burden is light (Matthew 11:28-30).

7

My Children, My Heirs—My Family

The consequences that result from the choice of abortion are never private. In fact, a woman's choice will become very public and affect everyone concerned. Some men will suffer great emotional pain after an abortion, especially if it is done without their consent or knowledge. Anger and rage fills them. They feel helpless and left out of the loop as the provider and protector of their child, and they feel their rights as a father have been taken away from them.

I stand before you as a man who loves his family and has honored his marital vows for the first 12 years of marriage. It all started so innocently. I married my childhood sweetheart after we both graduated from college. She went into accounting and I entered the business field. Those first few years of marriage were a period of establishing and building our new family. We became the proud parents of three beautiful children, two sons and one daughter. How I loved them. I had dreamed and hoped for two more children, for I thought our family would then be complete. You see, I had come from a large family, and I wanted my children to have the fun and company I had as I was growing up.

During this time, I became the owner of a highly successful business, which eventually spawned another successful business. Pouring all my time and energy into my businesses left the child-rearing and household responsibilities to my wife. She oversaw all the expenses at home, took care of the children, and was the perfect hostess when we entertained, which was quite often.

Eight years into our marriage, my wife became pregnant with our fourth baby. I was so excited and happy about the soon-to-come new addition to our family. Three weeks after the announcement of her pregnancy, however, I was hit by shocking news. My wife had aborted our baby without telling or asking me. I couldn't understand why. It was totally incomprehensible to me. I wanted our baby! We were financially well-off. Why would she do such a horrible thing without consulting me?

As I waited for her to explain, anger started to rise within me. My wife calmly explained that she was physically and emotionally drained. She couldn't handle a fourth child, given that our babies were all less than two years apart. A new baby would mean she would be dealing simultaneously with four children under the age of 7. I listened to her reasoning. I tried to be the understanding husband, but it was hard for me to even comprehend.

At that point, I was too busy to think about it or dwell upon it. I was running two corporations, and I was working over 70 hours a week. The priorities of my businesses took precedent over all situations on the home front.

Then, a year later my wife got pregnant again. Once again she made the same horrible choice to have an abortion, and once again I was not involved in the decision. Thus, our fifth child was aborted. This time I became physically angry with her because of her selfishness. We fought with heated and ugly words. She screamed at me, "It's my body, and this was my choice!" She accused me of never being home for her or the children. She complained that life was wonderful and sweet for me because she had all the responsibility of running the household and the children, and all I had to do was pay the bills. She said she needed more help and more emotional support from me, and she stated that it was obvious to her that my true wife, children, and family were my two businesses—not the people living in my home!

"What about us?" she screamed. "We need your attention, we need your time, we need your love, and we need you! We have enough money and enough stuff; we need *you!*"

The first words that ran through my mind were, "Look how hard I have worked for you, look what I have provided you with." I stressed how much I loved her and the children. I had worked hard so they could have a beautiful and rich life and never want for anything. How could she not see this? And, as I thought of those hateful words—"You just pay the bills!"—I grew increasingly angry.

I had been faithful to my wife for the first 12 years of our marriage and suddenly I realized that I didn't really know who this woman was. Who was this woman I was married to, this woman I came home faithfully to each night? Who was this woman who now held so much anger and rage against me because she considered me to be an absentee father and husband?

How could she think that? I had provided a 22-room mansion, and, in return, she had killed two of my babies! All I could see every time I looked at her were my two dead babies, my heirs. Yes, it made me angry, just as angry as she was with me for not being there for her. It was this anger that eventually destroyed our marriage.

Fifteen years have passed since that tirade of accusations exploded in our home. Yes, we are still married, but in name only. Following that outburst, we both started to lead separate lives, only coming together for family and social events.

We sleep in separate bedrooms. We are civil and courteous to each other and forbearing of one another. I lead my life and she leads hers. The years go by as we sit silently in our anger and rage. Our lives are so empty and devoid of love. Yes, we are still married—a marriage that has lasted 27 years.

I admit that I have had to seek other ladies for solace, while my wife involves herself with the children and her many charities. She's a good mother, a good woman, and I only wish that she had never made those deadly choices. It's very possible that our lives and our marriage could have been different.

It's been a long time to be so angry, but I just can't bring myself to forgive her.

God, please help me! This is no way to live.

Abortion is a decision that doesn't just affect the woman. It is a choice that also affects the father. He may have been the one who demanded and coerced the woman into the abortion, or he may have been the one who stood silently by as the choice was made, without even being part of the decision-making process, and told about it only after it was an accomplished fact. In either case, the husband becomes conflicted, despondent, and angry.

The views of both husband and wife become perverted, and their perspectives are tossed upside down. Deep down in their hearts, men sense the death of their baby, and they may suffer from the symptoms of Post Abortion Stress—just as much as women do.

8

Is It My Problem? I'm Only a Kid!

DID I HAVE TO KNOW?

The choice to abort a child will not only affect your present life; it will continue to haunt you throughout your future life as well. I only wish that someone would have told me of the consequences an abortion would have on me and the future generations. Abortion will affect and destroy the happiness of all of your future relationships, your future family, and your future children—indeed, your future in general. The aftermath of an abortion causes a generational affect as the little children of the next generation suffer the pain from the deadly choice made by their parent(s).

This is Janice's story.

I still recall that one Saturday morning when my mom and I got ready to do our "girl thing." We were going to go shopping. I was only 12 years old on that disturbing day when my mother opened up to me. She had tears in her eyes as she poured her lonely heart out to me. She was in search of some comfort, love, and reassurance, for she was all alone with her regrets, her pain, and her life-changing decisions. What my mother told me would change my perspective about my parents forever.

She shared with me that she had experienced more than one abortion prior to my younger brother's birth. To be exact, she had had four abortions. Until that admission, I never knew why my parents had spaced my little brother and me so many years apart. There is a ten-year age difference between us. Then a thought hit me: *my baby brother almost wasn't born and almost wasn't part of my life. I thought, Why did she decide to keep him? And did she also consider aborting me?*

Then my mother complained about how my father was so selfish, how she couldn't take birth control pills because they made her sick, and how he was never there for her emotionally. She told me that he worked such long hours, blah, blah, blah...

Did I need to hear all this? Did I really have to be part of her secret pain? I was only 12! Even though I empathized and felt sorry for my mom, I could not help but be upset and disappointed at her for being so helpless and irresponsible. After all, it takes two to procreate.

Another thought that kept hitting me was the fact that it had happened to her more than once! You would think that someone would learn after the first time and then take the necessary precautions to avoid another "accident"! But that was not the case with my mom. She then proceeded to tell me the reason why she had kept my baby brother. The doctor told her that it would be unsafe to perform another abortion, because it could be detrimental to her health.

Even now I get upset when I think about how she continues to make herself out to be the victim of my father's selfishness, yet still has not come to the realization of her own wrongdoings! It's as if she was so helpless and couldn't stand up for herself and take control of her own body!

True, in our Chinese culture, the woman tends to be submissive by nature and accommodating to the male dominant figure. In my mom's eyes, her role to my father was to be the "good wife" who cooked, cleaned, had his children, and took care of the home front. In my father's eyes, his role was to work and provide for my mom and the children.

My mother had been very dependent on my father in the process of coming to the United States. She came with a working visa in order to be with my father, who was at this time sponsored by his company to work in the U.S.A. Although proficient enough in English to get around and communicate, it was still not her first language. She had placed herself in a disadvantaged position. By her nature, she is very cynical and not trusting of other people, with the exception of my father. She thought she could trust him.

The things she told me continue to enrage me today. I am angry at my mom for being so weak and helpless, for blaming my father for the position *he* had placed *her* in. I don't see this solely as my father's irresponsibility and fault. I believe that she is just as guilty for allowing my father's actions. Why did she permit such irresponsibility? She had acted just as stupidly as my father.

Nowadays, the aftermath and repercussions of these abortions still float around us and are still being experienced by our family. My mom constantly cries and complains about her health issues and how the abortions have weakened her body, causing all her aches and pains. She complains to me and nags me, but does not do so to my father. Why me? She never says anything to my dad, because she doesn't want to "rock the boat." So, instead, she rocks *my* boat and takes all of her frustrations and anger out on *me*.

I'm the opposite of my mom in the way I deal with frustrations. Instead of remaining silent and not venting to the person who is aggravating me, I speak my mind and confront the person, whether directly or indirectly, in order to address the underlying issues. This holds true regardless of who the person is or what the situation is. I don't like to boggle and bury things deep inside of me.

My mother's situation frustrated me and it still angers me to this day. Perhaps this was why, during my temperamental adolescent years, I would get myself heatedly involved between my bitterly enraged parents whenever they would separate. I would argue with them, at them, and for them. Since they could not confront each other, I was the one who vocalized the frustrations and the anger between them.

They had separated a total of three times, and each time it made me extremely angry! Neither one could or would take responsibility for his or her own actions. They would vent their feelings, then place me in the middle, as the referee or mediator. I felt like screaming, "Hey! I'm the kid here, not the adult!"

This just was not fair! Couldn't they see how their deeds and actions affected my brother and me? Why couldn't they get past their differences, their anger, their mistakes, and move on in life? Why couldn't they resolve their unforgiveness?

Instead, they harbored deep resentment toward each other. Their indifference and anger often flared, and I was the one who was held hostage by their emotions and actions, because I had to live in their war-torn house.

I'd cry, "Why me?! God, please help my parents and please help me."

GROWN UP

We, as parents, need to be the adults in our family and try not to involve our children in the private wars we may have with our spouses. We have to learn to resolve differences with our mates, learn to communicate with each other, and determine to deal with the anger and indifference in our relationships.

We must learn how to forgive and love each other, and not be so selfish. If we cannot resolve the differences, then we need to get professional counseling to help deal with and get through the stormy times in life. We have to be responsible for all of our actions so that we can resolve our problems and have peace within our lives. This is not just for us, but also for the well-being of the family unit and for all future generations, as well.

I've expressed these ideas in my song, "Daddy, Help Mommy Make Me Her Choice" in which the baby cries out to the daddy and says:

> Just love my mommy and help her, daddy,
> To make me her choice.
> Please listen, daddy, you know I love you so.
> Please forgive my mommy, and I want her to know
> That there is still a chance that she could change her mind
> And choose to let me live.
> I know that she would find she'll love me too.

Cheryl Chew©

IF ONLY

If the fathers would only love the mothers of their children as Christ loved His Church (His Bride), there would never be any abortions; for Christ loved, treasured, cherished, respected, and honored His Bride to the point of laying down His life for her.

> *Love is patient, love is kind. It does not envy, it does not boast, it is not proud. It is not rude, it is not self-seeking, it is not easily angered, it keeps no record of wrongs. Love does not delight in evil but rejoices with the truth. It always protects, always trusts, always hopes, always perseveres. Love never fails...* (1 Corinthians 13:4-8).

> *Husbands, in the same way be considerate as you live with your wives, and treat them with respect as the weaker partner and as heirs with you of the gracious gift of life, so that nothing will hinder your prayers* (1 Peter 3:7).

Husbands are told to understand their wives, to respect and honor them, and to share the grace of life with them so that their life and prayers will not be hindered. They are reminded that they are the heads of their families. Wives are told to love, respect, and honor their husbands.

Are you both doing what you ought to be doing? Are you taking care of, loving each other, cherishing, respecting, encouraging, and supporting each other? Are you communicating your desires, your needs, your expectations, and your problems and fears to each other? How are these needs being communicated? Are these issues being communicated in a loving, gentle, and quiet way, or are they released in a shouting, threatening, degrading or demanding way?

Our individual lives are not just about "me, myself, and I." They are about sharing life together and loving one another. Marriage is about commitment and building a life together. Proper understanding of what love is and what good relationships are will help build a strong marriage. This, in turn, will build strong families, which will build a strong community, and ultimately a strong nation.

What is the foundation of your life and relationship built upon? Is it built on self? If so, it will self-destruct before your eyes. Or is it built upon good principles and precepts, and on the truth that has lasted for centuries?

9

By Grace You Are Saved

MARY'S STORY

As I was singing "Happy Birthday" over the telephone to my oldest daughter, Damali, on her 30th birthday, the phrase "By grace you are saved" suddenly filled my heart and mind. Indeed, it overwhelmed me and consumed the deepest part of me. Then feelings of sadness entered in and began to permeate the very air I was breathing. My body began to shake, and I had to take hold of myself and not let my thoughts drift back to the past.

Damali lived 3,000 miles away. I had not seen her for quite some time, and I greatly missed her. The last time she came for a visit, the reality of my love for her was easy to see as we interacted with each other. She had become a true survivor in spite of the hard times we had endured together as mother and daughter for 30 years.

I reflected on the many times when she had counseled and encouraged me. Damali was my own personal cheerleader who proudly proclaimed how I was such a great mother in spite of my own lack of belief in what she would say about me. I give thanks to the Lord for giving her to me.

After I hung up from her birthday phone call, I found myself behind closed doors, weeping and praising God for His divine intervention in Damali's life and my own. Not a single day goes by when I do not think about my daughter, our life together, and the experiences I'm about to share.

Thirty-one years ago my life did a complete turnaround, and it is still spinning today. I had just graduated from high school. My primary focus was on attending college away from home and being away from my childhood sweetheart, Vince.

I grew up in the projects of New York City and graduated from an all-girl's Catholic high school. I was accepted to a state university, which was a major accomplishment for me. It was a period of my life when there were many celebrations related to my accomplishments, giving me and my family reasons to sing, dance, eat, and drink.

My mother was filled with happiness and great expectations for me. She was proud and grateful that I was the center of attraction. In fact, I was chosen to provide the entertainment at one of the many activities related to graduation. We danced and sang at the Waldorf-Astoria Hotel, and it was a time of mixed emotions ranging from anxiety to exhilaration.

However, a deep and dark feeling of sadness began to take root deep inside of me, and these were feelings that I felt I could not reveal, not even to Vince. He was so proud of me, and he promised that our love for each other would weather all distant storms. We sealed our love with child-like intimacy over and over again throughout our five-year-long relationship. We took pride in the fact that there had not been any slipups along the way.

We had been violating the laws of God for at least five years and so we made certain that we would always make time for Saturday afternoon confession at church. When our parents would ask us about the physical aspects of our relationship, we would casually lie and deny any misbehavior, telling them, "We've never gone all the way."

Our lies, however, would soon be revealed, and the timing of this disclosure could not have been worse. A month after graduation I discovered I was pregnant, and I was supposed to leave for college in just a few weeks. "Oh, God, why now?"

In a panic, I thought, *What am I going to do?* I tried to perform an abortion myself, but to no avail. Finally Vince and I decided to go to a nearby abortion clinic that was owned by a well-known doctor. We made an appointment, and the date for the abortion was set by the clinic to take place on my 18th birthday. Boy, what a birthday surprise and gift this would be!

Vince drove me to the clinic that morning and made sure I was settled and checked in. He promised to pick me up when it was over and said that he would be waiting outside the clinic for me. Business was booming for the doctor and his clinic. I was not the only one who was scheduled for an abortion on that fateful day. Eighteen other young girls and ladies had also arrived for their scheduled abortions that morning, and still others had to be turned away!

My mind was set on the fact that this was my 18th birthday. It was also the birthday of my dad, who had passed away two years earlier. Those were my thoughts as I was being "prepped" and as I was relocated to a waiting area.

The waiting room was actually part of a huge room that was partitioned off by curtains into three areas: a waiting area, a recovery area, and a surgical area. I was frightened, but I tried to downplay the reality and seriousness of it all. Some of the girls began to make conversation with one another, but I sat away from the group. I watched and listened as the other girls began to bond with each other. They shared their bad experiences—stories of how and why they were there—and this gave them a common bond of sisterhood in a sad situation.

I sat outside of their circle, and they didn't even try to draw me in. I just didn't fit in; I knew it and they did too. The group leader was a tall, slim, dark-skinned sister who became the center of attention. She reassured the others that they had nothing to fear. She said, "It is going to be a breeze. Girls, we will be out by noon and at the disco by nine!" She ought to know. She had just been through this same procedure in March and she was just fine.

They performed the abortions in groups of threes. I watched as the trios made their way into the narrow area where the procedures were performed. The curtains were drawn and I could hear the sound of the suction machines. The deadening sound of life being sucked out. This was the "music" I heard as I waited for my turn to come.

As I watched for the curtains to open, I realized that the preceding three abortions had been accomplished, and now it would be someone else's turn. The ladies were rolled out of the curtained area into the recovery area in another section of the room.

As I waited, I could see the others in the recovery area. The assistant would come along and awaken the ladies shortly after they were taken to the recovery area. Some moaned and others vomited, and this gave me an idea of what to expect. My turn would soon approach, for there were now only two groups in front of me. I was beginning to look forward to getting this thing over with. I began to see beyond the reality of this day, as hints of sunlight began to find their way into the dimly lit room. I thought, *Yeah, girl, get over it, you have a life to live.*

As I sat there waiting, somehow I didn't feel wise and mature anymore. Everyone had always thought I had everything together, that I was always the counselor, and now I was the one who needed to be counseled. In my heart I cried out, *God, help me!*

My mind drifted back to recent events, and I recalled how receptive Vince had been to the idea of an abortion. His new 1974 Mustang and budding music career were what he was thinking of more and more. He had hinted at the idea that after the abortion we should reexamine our commitment to each other, but I wasn't sure what he meant by this.

I kept sending positive messages to myself: *Yes, girl, just get it over with; you have a life to live.* Suddenly, however, my thoughts were abruptly interrupted.

A woman's voice was shouting, "Wake up, Ms. Ernestine. Come on; get up. Honey, it's over. Wake up, get up now. Miss Ernestine! Everybody's gone in your group. Aren't you hungry? Miss Ernestine! MISS ERNESTINE!"

My attention shot over to the recovery area where Ernestine was located. She was the girl who had been telling us not to worry. Then a chilling announcement: "Code blue! Alert!" In response, the nursing staff ran hurriedly about in a frenzied effort to get emergency life equipment to the scene in order to revive Ernestine.

Three of us were still waiting for our abortions, and we began to panic. I impulsively started to walk over to the lifeless girl, thinking of my recent medical internship skills. One of the nurses stopped me and told me to go back to the waiting area. Suddenly I was paralyzed with fear, and I was unable to move for several moments. My mind was filled with thoughts of confusion, horror, and what I should do now. I was truly terrified.

Then I heard a voice within me that said, *"Flee!"* I searched anxiously for an exit and frantically looked for my clothes. I threw them on, and ran like crazy for three blocks, only stopping when I saw Vince on the corner. He was with his friends, and they were bumping loudly to the music from his car radio as he showed off his new vehicle.

I fell into his arms and cried hysterically. As I told him what had just happened, he held me tightly. Deep in my heart I knew that somehow all the events of this day were not mere coincidences.

It came to me that this day—my birthday, my deceased dad's birthday, and Ernestine's last day on earth—was a day that had been ordained by God. Come what may, I reasoned, the show will still go on, and the little precious who-so, the baby growing inside of me, was destined and purposed to live. Tragically, someone had to die so that Damali could live. "Wow!" I thought. *"God truly loves me so much, and His plan for me and my baby will surely come to pass."*

Dear Lord, thank you so much for interrupting our self-destructive paths. At times, you have to sharply wake us up to the plan, purpose, and love you have for us. God, you care for us more than we will ever know.

Happy birthday, my precious Damali.
And thank you, dear Lord,
For my precious birthday gift—
A beautiful lifetime gift of love and life.

The life and breath of people come from God (Isaiah 42:5 - paraphrase mine).

10

Weeping May Endure for a Night

CONSUELO'S STORY

I met Consuelo in 1996 when she first came into my bridal shop to buy her wedding gown. It wasn't until February 2002, however, that our friendship actually began; that is when she returned to my shop to visit and say hello. I thank God for the gift of her friendship, encouragement, love, and understanding.

Consuelo is a beautiful and gifted woman of God and this is her story.

It was in 1974 when the Lord showed Himself to me in a very profound, loving, and caring way. He showed me His understanding heart. I was a single mom and was pregnant again, and the man who I thought loved me and wanted to marry me had only given me false hopes and lies. He hurt me so terribly, and the sadness and pain I felt in my broken heart was more than I could bear. This all weighed so heavily upon me. I wanted to tell someone because I needed help. I needed someone who could listen to my crying heart.

So I talked to a few family members about my pregnancy and my desperate situation. Instead of them responding with understanding and helpful hearts, they scorned and ridiculed me. They said that I was a shame to my little boy and my family. Their hurtful words cut into my heart so deeply, and so did their bitter faces, which revealed the anger they had for me. All this made me feel even worse. Oh, how alone I felt! Day after day, and night after night, I would cry and cry. No one was there to comfort me or hold me. I had my little boy, and I knew he loved me, but still the pain and shame remained. This ugliness in my life had overtaken me to such an extent that I couldn't see any light or rays of hope on the horizon.

The overwhelming pressure that was caused by my lover leaving me, being a single pregnant mom, feeling so alone, and being attacked by my family just pushed my thoughts to only one solution: I had to get rid of this baby, so I reasoned that an abortion was the only answer.

It seemed that an abortion had to be the only way out of the terrible mess I was in. I couldn't have this baby, I reasoned, because I could barely support my son and myself. And the shame was too great. I couldn't handle that either.

In light of all these circumstances and feelings, I saw a doctor and was given an appointment at the hospital to have the pregnancy terminated. But in the early morning of the day of the scheduled abortion, I was still struggling very hard with my decision. I felt unsure of what I was about to do. I was crying hard, and the tears just kept coming. I had been brought up with a strong Christian background, so all kinds of emotions were stirring within me. As I sat on the edge of my bed struggling with this decision, the tears kept flowing down my face.

Suddenly I started crying out to God to help me, and somehow I now felt a tiny amount of faith lighting up my soul and spirit. I grabbed my Bible that I had rarely opened and said, "God, please help me; please help me. I know the answer's here, but I don't know where. Please show me."

I opened my Bible, and my tearful eyes fell upon these beautiful words: *"See now that I myself am He! There is no god besides me. I put to death, and I bring to life"* (Deut. 32:39). God was speaking directly to me. He helped me to see that He is the one who kills, and He is the one who makes alive. The power of life and death is within His domain, not mine, and it is His right, not mine, to take this baby within me.

In my darkest hour, God was there to hear me, to answer me, and to help me. Now I knew that my little boy and I would be fine. No amount of words can explain how I felt when God lifted this heavy load off me. All the feelings of rejected love, shame, and the inability to care for my baby, the baby that I thought I didn't want or need, were removed from me. God truly is there at the moment you need Him, at the very moment when you cry to Him for help.

On December 24, 1974, my beautiful baby daughter, Jennifer Joy, was born. As I held her in my arms, I felt so good and so complete. Her precious face and her tiny body spoke to me. My new baby was touching me with her love. As little as she was, I could feel her love for me, and I knew she needed me and I needed her. She became my bundle of joy, my sunshine, my gift of life, my baby girl. The Lord is so good. He saved me from making a terrible mistake, a mistake that would have lasted a lifetime. God helped me to make the right choice in keeping my baby. He turned my big problem into a blessing, and what a blessing, indeed!

I easily begin to weep when I think about what I would have missed out on had I aborted Jennifer Joy. What would life have been like if the Lord didn't help me when I cried out to Him? I would have never known my beautiful daughter. I would never have been able to enjoy loving her and the feelings of her loving me.

Likewise, my son would have missed out on so many things if he did not have his little sister. I would have never known the joy, the excitement of being her mom, and her being my daughter. God is so good! I would have never known Jennifer's kind and big heart, her friendship and laughter, and the sweet times we have spent together.

I am so blessed. It is because of God's understanding heart that He understood what I was feeling and what I was going through. It is because of His loving ears and eyes that I know my daughter, Jennifer Joy. If I would have aborted my daughter, I would never have known my wonderful son-in-law. And I would never have known my precious grandson and granddaughter either.

They are a *big* joy to me. How I love to hear their little voices as they call out to me, "Grandma." I love to touch their beautiful faces and feel the warmth of their hugs and kisses. They make me laugh and smile, and they bring tears of joy to my heart, for they are God's miracles, just like their mother, Jennifer, is. They wouldn't even exist if at first Jennifer didn't exist. If I would have gone through with that abortion, I would have missed out on some of the most beautiful blessings and rewards in my life—the joy of my precious family.

God is alive, and He's truly there when a hurting heart cries out to Him for help. Satan wants to rob us of wonderful blessings the Lord has for us. But if we just turn toward the Lord, He's always there to listen and to help us by showing His unconditional love to us. He doesn't look at our mistakes and His devotion and compassion toward us is always the same; it never changes. He doesn't love us or help us any less when we fail. I am so grateful to Him for that truth. And what we see as problems, impossibilities, and painful circumstances, God wants to turn into blessings.

The Lord is so good. In any terrible and dark situation we face, God will bring His understanding and loving heart and His light to us, showing us the way out of the ugly darkness into His saving arms. When this happens, we can smile again and feel joy again. Weeping may endure for the night, but joy comes in the morning. Every morning and every new dawn, our God is there to remove our weeping over the dark night of our past. Newness of hope springs forth with the dawning of each new day.

Love,
Consuelo Peterson

This poor man called, and the Lord heard him; he saved him out of all his troubles (Psalm 34:6).

A BRIEF NOTE FROM CONSUELO: Before I gave Cheryl the final approval to tell my story, I felt I first needed to speak to my beautiful daughter, Jennifer. I needed to find how she would feel about it, if she would be fine with me telling our story in this book. I was confident she would want me to, because I know she has a deep personal relationship with Christ.

These are Jennifer's words to me.

Hi, Mom,

I would love for you to share your story with others. It is more than a story. It is a testimony, one of many testimonies that the Lord has given *you because of the choice you made to give me life. I had always wanted a father, and I remember how you would tell me in my childhood and teen years that Jesus was my "Daddy" in Heaven, and that no matter where I would go He would always be with me. And with me He has always been! He was with me when I felt alone, when I ran from Him, and when I fell at His feet. He breathed my life into your womb, and I thank you with each beat of my heart. Mom, I love you more than you will ever know!!!*

    ~Jenn

Jennifer's story in her own words.

You did not choose me, but I chose you and appointed you to go and bear fruit—fruit that will last. Then the Father will give you whatever you ask in my name (John 15:15-17).

God chose me. He chose me to be a daughter who would be raised by a single mother who loved, adored, and worshiped the Lord. He knew from the womb that I would not know the love of a physical father. He knew from the womb that I would grow up and be the kind of woman my mother is, one who would boldly and faithfully worship Him with all her heart.

As I was growing up, I struggled with trying to understand my existence. I would cry for and long for a daddy, one who would wrap his arms around me, play with me, and tell me he loved me. I wanted a daddy who would call me his baby girl, his princess. As a child, I wondered why God didn't give me that desire of my heart. My older brother had a dad; why didn't I?

Every time loneliness entered my heart, my mother would try to fill the need and turn me back to the Lord. Over and over again she told me the story of how God wanted me so much that on the day when she was to abort me, He spoke to her through the Bible in order to keep me and save my life. Oh, how her faith grew. I smile now because the Bible represents the living Word of God, doesn't it? He used His living Word to bring life, my life, into existence.

As a child, I loved learning about the Lord and I loved going to church. Even though I felt like I didn't have a complete family, I was happy. I was filled with the Holy Spirit when I was just 7 years old. His presence in my life was so strong throughout my childhood.

Still missing a physical father, though, I leaned on the so-called love and affection of boys and men. During adolescence, I began to believe the lie that I needed to "feel" good about who I was. I loved being told that I was beautiful and popular. Was this my purpose in life? To be beautiful and popular? During this time, the Lord stayed faithful to me even when I turned away from Him.

He gently guided me with memories of my childhood—the times I spent with Him. He was truly becoming my "Daddy." He brought me back by reminding me of this scriptural truth: *"Before He formed me in the womb, He knew me"* (see Isa. 44:2) I was His.

While growing up, however, I struggled with giving my life to Him. I spent so much time in prayer and searching for what God wanted that I removed the need for men and was gaining spiritual strength. This strength weakened my spirit, however, because it came from my flesh.

At 22 years of age, I became pregnant with Aaron's child. We had only been together for six weeks. From the moment we met, I was in love with him. But six weeks for a guy in the Marine Corps doesn't necessarily mean love. Aaron had been raised in a Christian home with godly, loving parents, but what would he do in this situation? Would God honor me in spite of my sins? Would He allow Aaron to be a father to my unborn child? Would I be a single mom? God did honor me, and Aaron answered yes to fatherhood and yes to being with me.

Because of my close relationship with my mom, I was not afraid to tell her about my pregnancy. I knew I would have this baby. There was never a doubt in my mind about that. Abortion was never an option or consideration.

Even after eight years of marriage, I am amazed over how God truly works everything out in our lives for good. (See Romans 8:28.) The road Aaron and I chose was a difficult one, but God used that time to bring real strength into our lives. We met God where we were and He changed our lives. Today we live for Jesus Christ.

Every day I get to see the love of a father through my husband. He is a real daddy to Nicholas and Cauline, the kind of daddy that I always wanted. As I was growing up, people would tell me that the kind of daddy I imagined was too idealistic. They would tell me that no man could ever live up to my dreams. I'm happy to say that Aaron does every day.

So, you see, God also gave me a dad through my marriage. He is a father who represents truth. He moves with and waits on the Lord, and he trusts completely in the Lord. I'm speaking of my father-in-law, who has fulfilled the role that my heart had always longed for.

God even gave me a dad through my stepfather, who is a wonderful, loving friend to me. He is a kind, giving, and compassionate servant. Both of these men have Christ-like qualities, and they are also my children's grandfathers. How awesome! The Lord has blessed me more than I could have ever imagined!

He has given me double of everything that I thought I had been missing. Everything I envisioned in a father, I now have. I have always had those things with Christ, but now it is here on earth for me, as well.

When I ask many of my adult friends about their relationships with their fathers, they don't seem to share the same joy I have in my life today. God had protected me as a child even though I thought He had left me.

When my mom gave me the choice to live instead of aborting me, she gave me the choice to live out my purpose for Christ.

So what is my purpose in life? Why would God bring me into this world and leave me feeling so incomplete? Why am I here?

I am more than a conqueror through Christ who loves me. *"And we know that in all things God works for the good of those who love Him, who have been called according to His purpose"* (Rom. 8:28).

Christ has called me according to His purpose. I am His purpose. He loves me so much that He died for me so I would live with Him in Heaven. My life is complete in Him. Because my mom had the faith to make me her choice she is able to use this as a testimony. This is my testimony, and I've been able to share it throughout my life.

As a child, when friends were feeling alone, I would boldly tell them that Jesus loved them, and, as a child, I saw friends and their parents come to Christ.

As a teen, I told several girls who were pregnant not to go through with an abortion. In most cases, I was the only voice that was begging them not to. Even when I wasn't serving the Lord in those days, I knew the truth about abortion and the effects it would have on their lives forever.

As an adult, I kept my son when I got pregnant. Nicholas, my first-born, has a special relationship with God. He is only 7 years old, and he hears and talks with God. He prays for his friends and is known to have a tender heart.

My daughter, Kaelyn, is 6 years old and she has such a strong spirit. She worships the Lord with song. When she was 2 years old, doctors said she might never run or play sports, and they said she would have trouble reading and writing in school. The Lord healed her in an instant, and she now plays soccer, can read, and loves to draw. She is a wonderful artist.

Though our relationship began in sin, the Lord has given me a covenant marriage with my husband who is truly my best friend. When others said it would never work, the Lord said, *"It will work well and be used for My glory."* I'm thankful to be able to say that Aaron truly desires to be used by God.

Through my church, my neighborhood, and the school where I work I get to show love to kids. I have spoken and prayed with women and youths who have sex and drug addictions, have been victims of abuse, aborted their babies, given up their babies for adoption, and felt so alone.

Because of my mom, Consuelo, I am now able to share how God can heal and remove any pain in a person's life. The blood of Jesus Christ covers all. I am healed and I have seen His healing in the lives of others.

> *Therefore, if anyone is in Christ, he is a new creation; the old has gone, the new has come!* (2 Corinthians 5:17).

In your youth, middle age, or senior years you will always be "Daddy's little girl." Christ is the King, and you are His princess. No matter where you are or where you have been, you are His chosen. He called you by name, and He is calling the unborn child to live. If you have chosen "death" for your child, rejoice because your child is not dead, but he or she lives with Jesus Christ. Reach out to Him where you are. He has a purpose for you.

> *"You will be a crown of splendor in the Lord's hand, . . . no longer will they call you Deserted or your land Desolate. But you will be called Hephzibah [my delight is in her]. . . for the Lord will take delight in you* (Isaiah 62:3).

I live because He lives, and I love because He first loved me.

~*Jennifer*

11

A Pastor's Story—Post-Abortive Woman

REGINA'S STORY

The following is the story of a pastor named Regina.

"Sixteen years old and grown." That is how I would have described myself if anyone would have asked me. I took care of myself and helped to take care of my baby sister and my niece. I was an honor student in high school, had a job, and had boyfriend. According to my mother, I was a very responsible young lady. Then I became pregnant. Yes, pregnant!

What did I know about being a mother other than the fact that I loved my boyfriend and dreamed of one day being his wife and having his children. We were going to finish high school, go to college, get married, and live happily ever after. No one ever told me that sex before marriage was wrong. I never thought I would have to deal with pregnancy until after marriage. If you loved someone, how could sex with that person be wrong? No one told me that this "simple act" would "mess with me" for the rest of my life—and that which followed would damage me even more.

You see, the child I was pregnant with was never allowed to live. I had an abortion. Not just one, but two children were ripped from my womb within a year of each other. Oh, they were not called children back then. Instead, they were called "blobs of tissue not yet formed," according to the Planned Parenthood counselors. This "simple surgical procedure" would have me back on my feet in no time and I could continue on with my education and my life. Yeah, right!

Little did I know that my life would become even more complicated and dysfunctional as a result of this decision—if you can call it that, for it really was the only choice I was given. If the counselors really cared about me, they would have at least tried to discourage me from having sex, or at least would have asked me why I started. No one seemed to think that having sex was a problem. I was simply told to guard myself from pregnancy by using protection.

Protection! Who protects the babies?

Why wasn't I told about the side effects of abortion—the pain, the guilt, the fear, the anger, the condemnation, and the loss? Why wasn't I told the truth? No one told me about the depression, the hurt, the loneliness, the fatigue, the anxiety, and the suicidal thoughts that would follow me for years after the abortions. No one told me how I would react when I would see little babies in the mall, or that I would break down and cry if I passed the baby section of a department store. No warning was given to me that I would mourn the death of my children for many years to come and not understand what had gone on inside of me. No one told me I wouldn't enjoy sex again. I thought I was losing my mind!

I had severe intimacy issues, migraine headaches, and seething anger, much of which was kept under cover because I still did not know what was wrong with me. I rejected all those who loved me; yet I had sex with men in order to feel loved. Before I married, I told my husband that I could not love again. However, if I could indeed learn, he would be the one I would want to learn to love. So there I was—five months after dropping out of college, approximately one year after my second abortion, and I was getting married.

For many years I felt like a condemned woman who was simply waiting to die. I felt no one would mourn me and no one would bury me; they would just put me in a garbage bag and throw me away. Is this how one should feel for simply removing a blob of tissue from the womb? This feeling never occurred after my period, when I could see blood and a clot-like substance releasing from my body. What was different? I was not a medical doctor, but I knew something was wrong. *I had been lied to!*

I was told the abortion was supposed to allow me to finish school and later have a family. I was told the abortion was to make the "mistake" go away, and my boyfriend and I could still get married and have children. I was told after the abortion that I'd be on my way, free and clear, with no regret, because I was young and had my whole life in front of me. After the abortion I was told I might bleed a bit, just like having a period for a few days, and that I might experience cramping and weakness, but after that I'd be fine. *Lies, lies, and more lies!* Planned Parenthood lied to me, society lied to me, and the doctors lied to me.

> *There are six things the Lord hates, seven that are detestable to him: haughty eyes, a lying tongue, hands that shed innocent blood, a heart that devises wicked schemes, feet that are quick to rush into evil, a false witness who pours out lies and a man who stirs up dissension among brothers* (Proverbs 6:16-19).

I did not finish school. The relationship between my boyfriend and I went from bad to worse, and I lost intimacy not only with him but also with my friends and family. Can I blame all of this on the abortions? No. But much of what happened later in my life regarding my mothering instincts, my feelings and my lack thereof, my disconnectedness to my family, my depression, my self-hatred, these all came about as a direct result of the lies I believed from the counselors. This, in turn, resulted in my consent to abortion and sent me through a downward cycle of torment. Yes, I believe the abortions had much to do with all that.

After breaking up with my boyfriend and trying another relationship that did not work out, and dropping out of college, I returned home, only to get married five months later to a young man who went through hell with me.

Even after I received Jesus Christ as my Lord and Savior, I did not realize I had committed a great sin until I saw the film called "The Silent Scream." I was glued to the television set in horror, as I realized what had happened inside of my womb, not once, but twice! I cried profusely at the remembrance of what I had allowed to be done to my babies. They were not blobs of flesh, but real live, healthy babies. And for the first time I knew that what was warring in my mind and body was the death of my unborn children. My mind recognized the truth, and I began to acknowledge what had happened inside of me. I recognized the destruction that had occurred on the day I consented to such a horrendous act.

Then the healing began to take place.

Twenty-four years later, I am finally able to desire intimacy with my husband. We have four children. The oldest is 22 and the youngest is 13. It has taken 19 years for me to begin to learn how to bond with them and how to interact with them. I am learning to be a loving mother. I realize now that when I had the abortions, my motherhood seemed to have died along with my unborn children.

No one told me the truth.

Why is it so accepted in our society today to kill and to horribly murder by dismemberment the innocent lives that grow within us simply because we do not use self-restraint, practice self-control, or value the morals set by God? This is the cry of my heart now, for I now know the truth. Back in the days of my ignorance, I had unknowingly become a participant in genocide.

God, please help us. We know not what we did. Help us. Restore us. Heal us. Forgive us. Thank you, dear Lord.

> *I, even I, am he who blots out your transgressions, for my own sake, and remembers your sins no more* (Isaiah 43:25).

12

Woe to Those Who Call Evil Good

Woe to those who call evil good and good evil, who put darkness for light and light for darkness... (Isaiah 5:20).

I sat flabbergasted at the dinner table. Had her response to me about her stance on abortion been to justify her own actions, or to justify her daughter's abortion? How could she look me in the eyes and say that abortion is right? Where is the logic? Abortion is death. To abort is to cut off, to curtail, to end the life of the baby within a woman. Abortion at any stage of pregnancy, whether it is the first trimester or second trimester, is death.

Our conversation had started innocently enough. I had told her that I was writing a book on abortion that would be entitled, *Make Me Your Choice.* She flatly responded that she was pro-abortion, and she said, "I believe that it is OK to have an abortion in the first trimester of a pregnancy, because the fetus is still so small."

"How can you say it is right in the first 90 days and not later?" I asked.

She stated simply, "Because the baby is not completely formed."

"But," I countered, "at the point of conception, the moment your egg is fertilized by a sperm, it contains the plans for every detail of the baby's development, including sex, height, hair, and eye color. At the five-week stage of the fetus, one can see the baby's little arms with fingers, legs with feet and toes, and their eyes can be seen. By the end of the first trimester, the baby is completely formed. When a woman discovers that she is pregnant, it is usually at the six-week mark. So how can you establish a time line and say that abortion is OK up to a certain point?"

Where is the logic found in such an approach? When is it right to say, "What is wrong is right" just to justify one's own actions or deeds? We cannot, and we should not, for doing so is not telling the truth. To try to justify one's erroneous actions is to alter the truth and doing so is always a lie. Has society become so perverted and jaded that they will call what is evil good just to justify their own actions, their selfishness, and their ignorance of truth?

As this woman continued to state her position, her grandchildren came into the house. At that point I made mention of how beautiful and precious they were. After I said that, she could no longer answer the question. She just rose and walked away.

I wondered, after having children of her own and grandchildren, as well, how could she even think or try to justify that it is OK to take away a baby's right to life, to snuff out God's gift to mankind? Have we become a society that is so hardened and blinded by lies and selfishness that we will kill babies?

I have heard many people say, "Oh, it is just a glob or blob of tissue in the first trimester and not a baby, so therefore abortion is OK." In response to that statement, let me ask this: How many people, be they pro-choice or pro-abortion, have you heard say, upon discovering they are pregnant, "Oh, my! I just found out I'm having a glob of tissue." No, they will usually say, "Oh, my gosh! I just found out that I am pregnant and I'm going to have a baby." Even pro-choice advocates know in their hearts that there is life and a baby within them!

Let's get real, for truth is truth. We cannot justify our deeds in order to ease our consciences. I have had two abortions, and I know that I twice took a life, I know I have had to own up to my choice. I cannot justify my sins; only Jesus can do this for me.

I had another conversation with a young woman. She told me that she was pro-abortion, that a woman has a right to choose. She said, "After all, it's her body, her choice."

I asked her, "Have you ever had an abortion?"

She responded that it was "none of my business." My heart went out to her, for I could hear the remorse in her voice and feel her sadness. Her answer told me that she had had an abortion. If she really believed in abortion and in her conviction of choice, she would have answered with either a "Yes" or "No." Sometimes we choose and state our position on abortion just to justify our own secret deeds.

Wrong is always wrong. Wrong can never be right. Evil is always evil; it can never be good. If we attempt to change the truth to fit our situation by stating that a lie is truth, it still doesn't make it right. Truth does not work that way. Truth is always truth and it is good. Similarly, white is always white; it is not gray or black. A lie is a lie, and it is evil and bad, and it is harmful to one's state of being.

Unfortunately, we were brought up in a generation in which we were taught to believe that abortion is some sort of birth control. "Oh, you're pregnant! Just go down to the abortion clinic and have 'the problem,' 'the accident,' 'the inconvenience,' the baby taken out of you."

By the way, did they also let you know that you and your life will never be the same after the abortion? I remember when Billie Jean King came out in the 1970s publicly and told her story about her abortion and how she thought it was OK. The "women libbers" jumped on the bandwagon along with those who had had abortions.

Was this a declaration to ease their own consciences because of secret sins or their coerced choices? Try as I did to justify the sins of my two abortions, I just couldn't. I wanted to buy into the lie that it was OK to have an abortion so as to ease my aching heart, but I couldn't because I knew the truth and understood the truth. We cannot alter the truth just to ease our consciences or to fit our lifestyles.

When society starts to call evil good and good evil, then we need to stand up as a nation and stop the blatant defrauding of human values and life. If we do not do so, then we need to prepare and brace ourselves for a devastating, chaotic, and confusing time that will result in a generation so lost and confused that they will not know right from wrong. Such a generation would be so corrupt, so evil, so greedy, and so lost that society as a whole will eventually become corrupt and evil with no moral conscience, integrity, or standards.

Constant exposure to lies and sin desensitizes people with regard to their harmful effects, and people become so accustomed to lies, to a jaded lifestyle, and to a false way of thinking that it no longer registers as being wrong to them. Just like a cancer, it slowly, silently, and secretively invades the body and the mind until it festers and grows malignant. Then, before we realize it, we are at death's door. This is when evil will take over full control of the world, because the world will have become so blinded to the truth. We have to expose the cancer, so that we can treat it and eradicate it before it destroys and kills us.

Where do you stand, now that you know the truth? Are you standing on the slippery slope of lies, or are you standing firmly upon the truth? Where you stand as an individual will help to dictate the direction of our nation and our world. May the United States be brought back to the foundation that was laid by our founding fathers and take its stand upon the precepts and principles for which America was originally established and founded—on the uncompromising Word of God.

> Blessed is the nation whose God is the Lord, the people he chose for his inheritance. From heaven the Lord looks down and sees all mankind; from his dwelling place he watches all who live on earth—he who forms the hearts of all, who considers everything they do (Psalm 33:12-15).

> But the eyes of the Lord are on those who fear him, on those whose hope is in his unfailing love, to deliver them from death and keep them alive in famine (Psalm 33:18-19).

Help keep our country strong by building your life and thought processes on the Rock, the foundation upon which our founding fathers built the United States of America.

13

The Precious Gift of Life

VON'S STORY

I have known Von for over 20 years. Week after week I would go to her Ricca Donna Salon and sit in her chair as she would work magic with my hair so I wouldn't have a bad-hair day or bad-hair week. Whenever I was down, I knew a trip to her salon would improve both my appearance and my spirits.

As a hair stylist, she has heard much and listened very carefully to people as they unfold their lives to her. She believes that everyone is entitled to live the way they choose. She reasons that it is their life, their choice.

Up until three years ago, Von believed that it was a woman's right and choice to decide about abortion. She felt it was up to the individual woman, because it is her body and, therefore, her choice. Then Von became pregnant at the age of 39. Since then her opinion about abortion has changed radically.

Never thinking that she could or would ever get pregnant, thoughts of babies, parenting, and purpose had not entered into her thoughts or plans. In fact, she had a fear of childbearing, and even though she and Ray had been together for 17 years, the thoughts of marriage had never entered her mind. Also, Ray never wanted children; he was a confirmed bachelor and, at 50 years of age, he was ready to retire and enjoy the good life. Ray is a very successful attorney, businessman, and real estate investor, and Von is a very enterprising and successful businesswoman.

This is Von's story.

I never wanted a child because I had a great fear of childbirth. In January 2002, my older sister wanted another child, but couldn't get pregnant. She asked if she could have some of my eggs so that they could be implanted in her womb. Wanting to help, I went off the pill so I could give my sister my eggs.

I remembered Ray's father's request when he was on his deathbed 12 years ago. He asked me to marry Ray and have his children. I couldn't promise this to him, though, because I knew it would be a lie. I just didn't want kids.

In 2002 I went on a trip to Vietnam for two weeks, and while I was on that trip, I became extremely ill. I was vomiting and feeling sick all the time, and I thought I had caught some rare disease and that I was possibly dying. A week after I returned home I was still very sick, so I finally went to the doctor. His diagnosis, much to my surprise, was not some dreaded disease. It was morning sickness! I was pregnant!

When I shared the news with Ray that evening, he couldn't believe my words. His first reaction and remark was: "What! That doctor is stupid. He doesn't know what he is talking about. He can't be right. Possibly the pregnancy test kit could be wrong. Von, go to another doctor and get a second opinion."

My man was very angry and emotionally upset. Ray didn't think he was ready for a child, and he said, "What are you gonna do about it? Are you going to get rid of it?"

I told him, "If anyone has to go, it has to be you!" At that time I had been with Ray for 17 years.

He grew very quiet and finally responded, "Von, if you want this baby, then you will have to be 100 percent responsible for it!" He was 50 years old at the time, and he felt he was too old to have children. Plus, he was so involved with all of his businesses that he did not want the burden of child-raising.

So we spent over $25,000 to remodel a suite in my building for my baby's nursery while I would work. Five weeks before the baby was born, we hired a nanny so we could train her. The day when Avalon was born, Ray held her in his large arms. As she put her tiny, precious head upon his neck, he fell instantly in love with her.

Three days after our return home from the hospital, Ray fired the nanny and took over the complete care of our baby while I went back to work in my salon four weeks later!

A month after Avalon was born, Ray asked me, "Can we have another child?"

Avalon is a true miracle. She has added so much joy and love to our lives. We give her a thousand kisses a day, and we thank God daily for her. When Avalon was a year old, I mentioned to Ray, "Just picture life without Avalon. If I had been a weak person and had let you coerce me into having an abortion, we wouldn't have Avalon now."

Ray replied, "I don't even want to think about it!" Tears rolled down his face as he envisioned what life would have been like without Avalon if I had given in to him. How ordinary, predictable, and uneventful our lives would be without our precious little one.

It is amazing how much love a little baby can bring into one's life. Ray is a changed man. Who would have ever thought he would take full care and responsibility of our baby and still run his business dealings from the home? Ray has become the perfect "Mr. Mom." In fact, he is "Mr. Super Mom." I am so blessed and happy! Avalon has truly changed our lives. She has added so much color to our world and given us so much joy and laughter.

We both love Avalon with all our hearts, and we now realize that children are truly gifts from God. Now we are hoping we will be blessed with even more children. Since Avalon was born, I have had three miscarriages, but I'm still trying. Even if we can't have another child, we know that God blessed us when He sent us this precious, beautiful miracle. He sent us a special "angel," and her name is Avalon!

When I went to my prenatal appointments, we would take pictures of Avalon via the ultrasound. I would study those pictures each month, and

I was surprised by how well-developed she was while in the womb. I could see her tiny hands, and I watched as she would put her thumb in her mouth, blink her eyes, and yawn. She was so precious, so delicate, and so beautiful! After looking, evaluating, and cherishing those precious photos, I realized how soon life is created and formed in the womb, and I knew that what was growing inside of me was not just a blob of tissue, but a complete and formed baby—a real, live human being. Now, obviously, my perspective on abortion has changed.

I realize and understand the preciousness of life and God's gift of life. I did not know or realize the horror of abortion until one day when I watched a documentary on television that showed babies in the womb. This film described how the babies can feel pain when the mother's womb is invaded with a probing instrument. They showed an ultrasound video in which the baby was trying to get away from the foreign object. I was shocked and horrified to witness such a scene!

At one time I was pro-abortion; now I am pro-life. How could I have made a choice to destroy the precious life of my baby and take away Avalon's right to live out her life as God intended her to live? To be so selfish and thoughtless towards God's beautiful creation, toward His gift of life, makes me want to cry now for all the aborted babies.

14

Father, Forgive Them, for They Know Not What They Do

JUDY'S STORY

Sometimes we become so blinded to the real truth that we don't know what we are doing. Because of fear, rejection, a need to justify, other needs or ignorance, we make choices and do things that we don't fully understand or comprehend that will cause us a lifetime of remorse. Sometimes out of the necessity of keeping a job or for some other reason, we numb ourselves to the sins we commit.

This is Judy's story.

I am a nurse. About 23 years ago I went to work in a private clinic where there were three doctors: a plastic surgeon, a family practitioner, and an Ob/gyn specialist. The first year I worked in the clinic was exciting because I worked with the plastic surgeon, assisting the doctor in all of his out-patient surgeries. I was fascinated by his surgical-enhancing procedures and I enjoyed being his assistant.

The following year, however, my supervisor transferred me to the Ob/gyn department and there I was to assist the doctor in all of his out-patient procedures, including D&Cs (dilation and curettage) and abortions.

During this time my duties involved preparing the patients for the procedure. I was instructed to counsel with them if they had any questions. If they were having an abortion, I was to reassure them about their decision by telling them it was all right and that "they were just getting rid of a blob of tissue."

My final duties were to clean up after the surgery. It would pain my heart and torment my soul when I would have to clean up after an abortion. There, at the end of the stirrup table, was a bin where the doctor would toss the small, crushed body parts of the fetus after he dislodged it from the mother's womb. I could see the bloody, tiny crushed bodies with their small arms, tiny fingers, and legs that sometimes got torn away from their bodies.

Seeing this procedure done several times a day, one can become immune and numb to the death of the fetus. In order to survive, I had to accept this aspect as just part of my job, not wanting to fully realize the consequences of what I was doing. I would go home at night and have nightmares, because I was the one who had to dispose of the little mangled and crushed bodies and place them in the incinerator.

Since these procedures were done under the veil of secrecy, there was no other way to dispose of the body parts but to burn them at the end of the day. I had to watch the doctor as he would insert the forceps into the cervix to puncture the uterus and then crush the fetus in his efforts to dislodge it from the womb. I felt so guilty when I had to collect the babies' body parts and then burn them.

Apprehension and dread would come over me each working day, and it was a challenge for me to get up in the morning because I knew what was in store for me. Depression would come upon me. My heart and conscience weighed heavily within me, for I knew the real truth.

It was during this time that I became pregnant with my third child. My husband was "fooling around" with another woman and this child was unplanned. I started to entertain the thoughts of abortion because I felt totally rejected by him. He told me he didn't want the child.

All I could think of at that time was *I need to self-abort this baby*. I had all the necessary instruments and drugs at my fingertips, and I had observed so many abortions, so I thought it would be easy to do.

Nobody would ever know and I could dispose of it in the incinerator. As the thoughts of abortion continually entered my mind, I was numbed to the reality of the living being within me due to the daily abortions that had become so routine in my mind and life. My conscience had been numbed (anesthetized) to the evil that I had participated in as a part of my job, rendering me incapable of thinking or reasoning soundly.

I bounced back and forth between two thoughts: *Should I, or shouldn't I?* The fear of God overcame me. Having been raised in a Christian home, I went to see my pastor. I told him of my predicament.

He told me that children are a blessing from God, and he prayed, "God, give Judy the strength to make the right decision and to endure and overcome everything that she is going through."

I thank God daily for the godly wisdom and prayer that the pastor gave me, for I chose to keep my little baby girl.

The Ob/gyn doctor I worked for said, "Judy, when you have your baby, I promise not to be drunk on that day; I will remain sober for your C-section." I was happy to know that he didn't want to make any mistakes concerning me or my baby.

I truly believed that the doctor drank excessively because deep down in his heart, he knew that he was taking lives through abortion, and this must have weighed heavily upon his conscience. It was only two years after the birth of my daughter that he died in a horrible automobile accident that had been caused by his drinking. After the birth of my daughter, I never went back to work in that clinic. Today my precious little girl is a beautiful young woman and a successful banker, and I thank God for her daily.

Since then I have prayed and asked God for forgiveness for my participation in all those abortions. I have also asked the Lord to be with all those ladies who had abortions and to help them through their difficult and tumultuous times. As I assisted those ladies in the clinic, I could feel their anger, despair, fears, frustrations, confusion, and depression.

> *This is what the Lord says: "A voice is heard in Ramah, mourning and great weeping, Rachel weeping for her children and refusing to be comforted, because her children are no more"* (Jeremiah 31:15).

Today I am working with terminally ill AIDS victims, and I'm also counseling hurting women who are going through life crises. My goal is to help them heal their pain through God and His Word, prayer, understanding, compassion, and love.

> He will respond to the prayer of the destitute; he will not despise their plea. Let this be written for a future generation, that a people not yet created may praise the Lord: The Lord looked down from his sanctuary on high, from heaven he viewed the earth, to hear the groans of the prisoners and release those condemned to death (Psalm 102:17-20).

There are many times in our lives when we have to make choices and take a firm stance, when we must do what is morally correct. We should never choose to do something only because we think we need to do it in order to survive.

There is never a need to compromise yourself in your work—there are too many other occupations, jobs, and positions available so that you will not have to do that. To do what is politically correct simply because of majority rule or out of pure necessity will harm your very being and conscience. It will contaminate your life and your way of thinking.

Is it worth the pain and heartache or nightmares that will result? The aftermath of a bad choice will chase you down and haunt you for the rest of your life. Think about it; is it worth all that?

15

As I Sit Here Silently

As I sit silently here in the county jail, waiting patiently for my six-month sentence to pass by, I've been reflecting upon my past. As I review my life, it is amazing to note how one's emotional state of being may become one's physical reality as it did in my case. How many years was I held hostage by my thoughts, my deeds, and my actions, and now I'm in an actual jail cell!

Six months in jail is nothing compared to the imprisonment that first started in my mind 20 years ago when I was a little girl. My father would whisper in my ear, "Now don't tell mommy or anyone else what you and I have done. If you do, they will not like you anymore, because mommy will think I love you more than her, but I love you both equally."

How could he tell me that he loved me? What he just did to me hurt me—it hurt me a lot. I tried to scream and cry, but he would muffle my screams with his big ugly hands. If this is love, I reasoned, I don't want any part of it.

This was what my childhood was like: one abuse after another. It caused me to become so angry and apathetic to life. I became like a zombie. I hated my father. I couldn't trust any man, because I thought of my own father sexually abusing me and how he said he did so out of love. I wondered what other men were like. Were they all like my father? Would they hurt and beat me? How could I ever trust a man? I had learned to associate men with brutality, pain, hurt, lies, lies, and more lies.

What did I know of life? My life had consisted of incest, violence, pain, and lies. Is this what life is all about? Is this normal? Do all little girls experience this? I wanted to scream, for it just didn't seem right to me.

Then, at 12 years old, I became pregnant; it was my father's baby. Mom and dad forced me to have an abortion. I hated my mother. She never stood up for me or protected me from dad. Why did she allow him to hurt me?

I remember when she took me to the doctor. She was so stoic, and her face was so stern and lifeless. Throughout the whole ordeal, she never said one word to me. It seemed as if there was no compassion in her.

As I look back on those days, I know living with dad was hard for her, especially during his alcoholic rages which took place almost daily. My father was a big man, and she was too small and frightened to stand up against him or to run away.

My mother had felt my father's fist slamming hard against her face and body many times. She was too fractured, too broken, too hopeless, and too scared to stand up to him. So she just took everything he dished out both to her and to me! Mom was numb to life and everything around her; she just existed from day to day, probably wondering if she was going to make it alive into the next day!

So as I grew up, I fell into one bad relationship after another. Those relationships were all very similar to our family relationships—abusive and violent. However, these kinds of relationships felt normal to me—the abuse, the coercion, the yelling, the backhand slaps across my face, and the fists against my body—all of this was everything I had experienced while growing up in my parents' house.

I thought, *God, is this what life is all about?* After falling in love with and being disappointed with so many different men, my perception of myself and my life became very warped. I felt ugly. I felt old. I felt used. I felt unclean. I felt shameful. I hated myself.

These men didn't want me or the babies we had conceived together, supposedly under the guise of love. Each of these five men in my life made me get abortions when I became pregnant. They threatened to leave me if I didn't have the abortions, and where would that leave me? Who else would want me? It was apparent that they didn't want me either, for if they had wanted me, they would have let me keep our baby. I must admit, however, that I did wonder if I truly wanted to bring a child into a hostile environment? For all these reasons, I felt I didn't have any other choice but abortion each time I became pregnant. In other words, the choice was made for me.

From the second abortion to the fifth, my life was very abused and out of control. I was heavy into drugs and alcohol—efforts to ease my pain, my nightmares, and my memories.

As I continued to reflect upon my past, I did not like what I saw. The pictures were too hideous, and the memories were too hard and sad. That's why I would disappear into the hazy fog of my heavy drug use and alcoholism. Those addictions would help to numb me and take away the ugliness, anger, and hatred that I harbored within me and found their way into the life that surrounded me.

But every time the drugs and alcohol would wear off, I found myself in that same dark hole again, and it was very hideous, cold, and ugly. Realizing this, I would keep myself constantly loaded—"hooked up"—so I couldn't and wouldn't feel the pain, the ugliness, the shame, and guilt. I was imprisoned by my memories and my thoughts.

Incidentally, the reason why I'm in jail as I write this is because of drugs and writing bad checks. I needed a fix, and I got caught by an undercover agent. So here I am today locked in jail in two ways—as a real prisoner and as a prisoner of my thoughts and deeds, but I must say that none of my misdeeds are as horrific and sad as the deaths of my five babies, which is a horror I relive every single day. Will I ever get a chance at motherhood again? Will I ever be happy? Will I ever find a man who won't hurt me, a man who will truly love me?

I now know that abortion is the killing of a baby. This realization hurts my mind and my heart every time I think of it, and there is not a day or night that goes by when I don't think of all my dead babies.

The nightmares and night terrors that I experience are beyond description; they are filled with darkness, a fiery inferno, dead babies, incessant howling, screaming, and crying. Those are the reasons for my extreme drug addiction and abuse. I had tried everything I could think of to ease, block, and numb the pain I felt deep within, and to shut out the menacing voices that screamed inside my head.

The abortion clinic workers told me not to worry about it because they were just removing "a blob of tissue," and I wouldn't feel anything. However, the pain after the third abortion was excruciating, and I had to be rushed to the Emergency Room after the third day, because I was bleeding excessively and running a high fever.

The ER doctor told me that I might have a perforated uterus, and if that were the case, they would have to do a hysterectomy. I discovered later that my uterus had not been punctured, but that the abortion clinic had left some of the "fetal matter" (parts of the baby) and part of placenta inside of me. Because of this, they had to do a D&C. I'm lucky to be alive today, for the doctor said if I had not come in when I did, I would have hemorrhaged to death!

I'm trying to pick up the pieces of my shattered life, but it isn't easy, and I don't know which way to turn. God, please help me! I never wanted to live this kind of life, the kind of life that I am now living.

But how do I get out of my quandary? Is there hope for a peaceful or happy life?

God, I need you! Please help me out of this hole that I have put myself in! And please forgive me.

> Praise awaits you, O God, in Zion, to you our vows will be fulfilled. O you who hear prayer, to you all men will come. When we were overwhelmed by sins, you forgave our transgressions (Psalm 65:1-3).

God is faithful to forgive us of all of our transgressions when we confess our sins to Him. (See 1 John 1:9.)

We need to look to God for wholeness and healing for our body, soul, and spirit if we want to get past our desperate situations. We need to have an attitude of receiving and accepting God's love, forgiveness, and peace and we need, also, to forgive ourselves and others, for it is in the forgiving of ourselves that we will find the much needed peace we are searching for. Never forget that God always forgives you when you ask Him to! He is always there for you, just call out His name…Jesus!

16

God's Unlimited Forgiveness: Matthew 18:22

CYNTHIA'S STORY

I believe we all have a story to tell. Mine is no more special than anyone else's except that it is unique to me and in accordance with God's divine design, purpose, and plan for my life.

The topic of abortion is still very much a controversial one. However, it is the very topic of my life. I have had six abortions. I have been pregnant a total of 15 times. From those pregnancies I have given birth to seven children—all boys. I had twins who died not long after their birth and my two youngest children were born out of wedlock. Therefore, I have five living children who range in age from 25 to 6 years old.

I did not grow up in poverty. While I was a blessed child, materialistically speaking, I struggled desperately with my mental, physical, and emotional well-being as I endeavored to discover my personal identity. The experiences of sexual molestation as a child and the rape I experienced as a young woman left me fragmented, and those experiences instilled and perpetuated self-defeating and disruptive behavior patterns in my life, patterns which lasted well into adulthood.

With the consent of my parents, I enlisted into military service at the early age of 17—soon after my high school graduation and not long after my first abortion. When I was 16 years old I became pregnant and, at the insistence of my parents, I endured a second-trimester abortion. By the time I reached my 18th birthday, I was married. Being too young and immature, the marriage ultimately turned into a nightmare and did not last long.

By the age of 23, I was already into my second marriage and I gave birth to my second son. I had three abortions during my second marriage. Then I was divorced from my second husband after I had the last two abortions. I justified this by convincing myself that having the last two abortions was the best solution for my problem.

At the time, I considered myself a "Christian" and I was serving in the church. I believe this is just one example of how many women become ensnared by the lies of the enemy (the devil). The belief that the "church" is going to respond to our pregnancies outside of marriage with persecution and condemnation tends to weigh more heavily on us than even the thought of sinning against God does.

Deciding to have an abortion in the hope of avoiding the negative comments and glares of disgust from others simply compounds our sin against God. After the abortion there is guilt because of the pregnancy, and even greater guilt and shame for terminating the pregnancy. The bondage leads to greater captivity as the chains tighten around us and the daily torment worsens. At least it did in my case.

In spite of what other people would say about me, at some point I determined and decided that doing what was right in the sight of God was far better than repeating years of torment and returning to alcohol as a means of self-medication for anesthetizing the emotional pain I had experienced from it all. I also found it much easier to ask God to forgive me for the fornication than to have to ask for forgiveness for both the fornication and abortion.

Through reading the Word of God I discovered that taking God at His Word and believing it is true was the key, and I realized that this was the same way I had received salvation. It is by faith that we receive the grace of God and His forgiveness. Eventually, I realized that I had not truly believed that I had received God's forgiveness, and I was actually saying that what Jesus did on the cross for me was not enough.

By faith I accepted the truth of His redemption and forgiveness in my life. This understanding completely changed how I thought, and it caused a paradigm shift in my mind. I experienced spiritual freedom in my mind, soul, and spirit.

It was then that I knew Jesus Christ had, in fact, accomplished more than enough for me by His death on the cross. Romans 5:8 puts it well: *"But God demonstrates his own love for us in this: While we were still sinners, Christ died for us."* This verse was a valuable nugget that I deposited in my heart. I still meditate upon its truth and upon this verse, as well: *"We love because he first loved us"* (1 John 4:19).

Today, of course, I realize the abortions I underwent were in direct violation of the Word of God. I sinned against God, whether knowingly or unknowingly. I now know and understand that abortion is clearly wrong because it causes a life to be terminated. The life that is terminated by an abortion is not a life that human beings have created, but it is a life that God has created. We know this from reading Psalm 139:13-14: *"For you created my inmost being; you knit me together in my mother's womb. I praise you because I am fearfully and wonderfully made; your works are wonderful, I know that full well."*

I was entrusted by God to be the carrier of a life. He put life within me through the reproduction process and I aborted that life—His creation. No one has the right to destroy what God has created. Nevertheless, God knew the end from the beginning. He already knew that I was going to have those six abortions; even so, Jesus went to the cross for me.

Psalm 90:8: *"You have set our iniquities before you, our secret sins in the light of your presence."* When I realized that God is all-knowing and that it is useless to continue trying to hide from Him, I cried out to Him. I confessed my sins to Him, and I repented of all my sinful choices and actions.

> *If we claim to be without sin, we deceive ourselves and the truth is not in us If we confess our sins, he is faithful and just and will forgive us our sins and purify us from all unrighteousness. If we claim we have not sinned, we make him out to be a liar and his word has no place in our lives* (1 John 1:8-10).

My two younger sons are living testaments to my repentance from abortion, because they were born out of wedlock. Assuredly, by the time of their arrivals I was a more mature Christian and knew better than to engage in sex outside of marriage. Nevertheless, the old me would have attempted to cover my sin of fornication and shame by having an abortion.

But because I had received God's forgiveness and knew His lovingkindness personally, the challenge to abort or not to abort had been removed from me. I knew that giving birth, in spite of the persecution or comments that might come from those who did not understand why I would have another child at almost 40 years of age, was the only proactive choice I could possibly make.

Psalm 103:3 says, "[The Lord] *forgives all your iniquities and heals each one of your diseases.*" Psalm 65:3 (AMP) emphasizes the impact and power of God's forgiveness in our lives: "*Iniquities and much varied guilt prevail against me; [yet] as for our transgressions, You forgive and purge them away [make atonement for them and cover them out of Your sight]!*"

Another important passage in the Book of Psalms shows what God's forgiveness in our lives will do:

> *What happiness for those whose guilt has been forgiven! What joys when sins are covered over! What relief for those who have confessed their sins and God has cleared their record. There was a time when I wouldn't admit what a sinner I was. But my dishonesty made me miserable and filled my days with frustration. All day and all night your hand was heavy on me. My strength evaporated like water on a sunny day until I finally admitted all my sins to you and stopped trying to hide them. I said to myself, 'I will confess them to the Lord.' And you forgave me! All my guilt is gone* (Psalm 32:1-5 TLB).

In short, I began to simply take God at His Word and began practically applying what the Bible said to my life. This is what James tells us to do: "*But be doers of the Word [obey the message], and not merely listeners to it, betraying yourselves [into deception by reasoning contrary to the Truth].*" (James 1:22 TLB).

Jesus came to give us life and to give it to us more abundantly. (See John 10:10.) The Bible declares that we who are in Christ will enjoy the liberty or freedom from sin and torment that comes to us when we rest in the perfect love of God. First John 4:18 assures us, "*There is no fear in love. But perfect love drives out fear, because fear has to do with punishment. The one who fears has not been made perfect in love.*"

Jesus died and was resurrected that we might know a life free from mental and emotional bondage and torment. Through this understanding, I had finally received a revelation that helped me understand that where the Spirit of the Lord is there truly is liberty. This truth is now settled in my spirit, because I know, *"...if the Son sets you free, you will be free indeed"* (John 8:36).

> *But when the goodness and loving-kindness of God our Savior to man [as man] appeared, He saved us, not because of any works of righteousness that we had done, but because of His own pity and mercy, by [the] cleansing [bath] of the new birth (regeneration) and renewing of the Holy Spirit, which He poured out [so] richly upon us through Jesus Christ our Savior* (Titus 3:4-5, AMP).

It is humbling to reflect back on my past, because as I do so, I see what the Lord has done in me, for me, and through me for His glory and for the benefit of others. It is even more humbling to be a living witness to His auspicious nature, which has been my greatest weapon of offense against the accuser of the brethren.

> *And they overcame him by the blood of the Lamb and by the word of their testimony, and they did not love their lives to the death* (Revelations 12:11 NKJV).

One of the most mind-renewing and inwardly transforming Bible passages that is engraved in my heart can be found in the writings of the apostle Paul.

> *For the love of Christ controls and urges and impels us, because we are of the opinion and conviction that [if] One died for all, then all died; And He died for all, so that all those who live might live no longer to and for themselves, but to and for Him Who died and was raised again for their sake. Consequently, from now on we estimate and regard no one from a [purely] human point of view [in terms of natural standards of value]. [No] even though we once did estimate Christ from a human viewpoint and as a man, yet now [we have such knowledge of Him that] we know Him no longer [in terms of the flesh]. Therefore if any person is [ingrafted] in Christ (the Messiah) he is a new creation (a new creature altogether); the old [previous moral and spiritual condition] has passed away. Behold, the flesh and new has come! But all things are from God, Who through Jesus Christ reconciled us to Himself [received us into favor, brought us into harmony with Himself]*

and gave to us the ministry of reconciliation [that by word and deed we might aim to bring others into harmony with Him]. It was God [personally present] in Christ, reconciling and restoring the world to favor with Himself, not counting up and holding against [men] their trespasses [but cancelling them], and committing to us the message of reconciliation (of the restoration to favor). So we are Christ's ambassadors. God making His appeal as it were through us. We [as Christ's personal representatives] beg you for His sake to lay hold of the divine favor [now offered you] and be reconciled to God. For our sake He made Christ [virtually] to be sin Who knew no sin, so that in and through Him we might become [endued with, viewed as being in, and examples of] the righteousness of God [what we ought to be, approved and acceptable and in right relationship with Him, by His goodness].… Laboring together [as God's fellow workers] with Him then, we beg of you not to receive the grace of God in vain [that merciful kindness by which God exerts His holy influence on souls and turns them to Christ, keeping and strengthening them—do not receive it to no purpose] (2 Corinthians 5:14-21 and 6:1 AMP).

If you read and meditate on this particular text of the Bible for one week, you will come to know, as I know, that I could easily end this testimony right here. I believe this is truly one of the greatest God-inspired writings. This passage gives us a look at the Great Commandment and Great Commission all in one revelatory passage. And since the apostle Paul was placed on assignment by the resurrected Savior and Lord, Jesus Christ, to compel the Gentiles to Himself, I do not know of any other place in the New Testament Scriptures that best reveals a summation of the Gospel of Jesus Christ to the Gentiles with the same intensity as we see in Second Corinthians 5:14-21 and 6:1.

How sobering it became for me to know how our Sovereign prevails in His calling and His leading by His Spirit; He has led me out of darkness and into His marvelous light.

First Peter 2:9 (AMP) states: *"But you are a chosen people, a royal priesthood, a holy nation, a people belonging to God, that you may declare the praises of him who called you out of darkness into his wonderful light."*

Peter goes on to say, *"Once you were not a people [at all], but now you are God's people; once you were unpitied, but now you are pitied and have received mercy."* This is clearly indicative of just how frail I am before the majestic God. But it is even more a testimony of His unfailing love for me. This realization births an all-encompassing revelation of my resolve to yield or surrender my will to His perfect will, and to allow God to be manifested as He is—the Preeminent One over every part of my life.

God's grace is so amazing. His love is without measure, and He lavishes it upon us who are His. Jesus said,

> *Come to Me, all you who labor and are heavy-laden and overburdened, and I will cause you to rest. [I will ease and relieve and refresh your souls.] Take My yoke upon you and learn of Me, for I am gentle (meek) and humble (lowly) in heart, and you will find rest (relief and ease and refreshment and recreation and blessed quiet) for your souls. For My yoke is wholesome (useful, good—not harsh, hard, sharp, or pressing, but comfortable, gracious, and pleasant), and My burden is light and easy to be borne* (Matthew 11:28-30 AMP).

Through my trials and tribulations that resulted from my errors, God has brought me full circle. He has planted me in an outreach ministry and anointed me to teach and minister to women who are facing the challenges involved with an unplanned pregnancy. He has equipped me to be a facilitator in post-abortion groups, and I counsel with women who are plagued by the post-abortive syndrome that many of us experience.

We serve an awesome God, and He is no respecter of persons. If you have not done so already, I pray that you will forgive yourself. Forgiveness begins when you ask God to forgive you. But it also requires that you forgive yourself. His Word says,

> *Then Peter came to Jesus and asked, "Lord how many times shall I forgive my brother when he sins against me? Up to seven times?" Jesus answered, "I tell you, not seven times, but seventy-seven time"* (Matthew 18:21-22).

Forgiving ourselves can be very challenging, to say the least. But God is love, and He waits with open arms to embrace us as we are. He knows that we cannot "fix" or restore ourselves or even our lives for that matter, apart from Jesus Christ.

God is more than able to give you a new heart, and He wants to put a new spirit in you. He promises: *"I will give you a new heart and put a new spirit in you; I will remove from you your heart of stone and give you a heart of flesh"* (Ezek. 36:26).

Once I decided to let go and let God be the Lord of my life, restoration began. Today I can honestly say, *"In my distress I cried to the Lord, and He heard me"* (Ps. 120:1 NKJV).

CYNTHIA CHINN, Founder of Women-Empowered Ministry

Christian Counselor/Facilitator

17

Never Alone

AMY'S STORY

In the following story you will discover what Amy learned through all the circumstances in her life.

At 18 I had a plan and a purpose. I didn't know the Lord, but I thought I knew myself. Like many seniors in high school, I enrolled in a junior college before graduating. As the pressure to decide about a career built up, I thought I would make a great social worker. I was never good at math or history, but I loved to work with people.

My boyfriend, Lee, was taking time off from college when we met. He had moved back home and I started seeing him at all the parties. I liked him right away because he was intelligent and funny, and he knew how to have a "good time." We made a great team. I trusted Lee with everything.

After graduating from high school, I enjoyed a summer that was full of parties and friends. When I started my general education classes in college, everything was going as I had planned. Well into my first quarter, I was struck with a severe flu, however. I was so sick to my stomach that I had to pull to the side of the road to throw up almost every morning. I ended up in bed for a whole week. My body trembled, and I ached from head to toe. My dad was really concerned about me, and I knew something was terribly wrong.

For several months, my sister, who was a newlywed, had been trying to get pregnant. I would go with her to the health department every time she thought she might be pregnant. She and I had already been there twice when she asked me to take the trip with her a third time. When we were at the counter she convinced me to take the pregnancy test, too.

That afternoon she and I walked out of the health department in tears. She was hurt that her test was negative, and I was destroyed because mine was positive!

I sat and cried with my sister for what felt like a year. Terrified and not knowing what to expect, I went to Lee, who was incredibly understanding and calm. At the end of our conversation we were faced with the thought that abortion seemed to be the "only way out" for us. We discussed other options, but didn't feel comfortable with anything else. At the conclusion of our highly emotional conversation, we determined we would not make a decision about it until after we had told our parents.

My father didn't take the news very well. My conversation with him ended on a note that I would prefer to leave in the past. In a very disappointed fatherly tone, he told me, "Your life will never be the same. You will never be able to truly experience life. How could you do this? What about your future?"

My relationship with my mother was strained at the time, as well. She asked me, "Well, what are you going to do?" At 18, I had no idea what I should do. I just knew that I hated being me and I couldn't imagine bringing a life into this world without any support or guidance. It just didn't seem to be the right thing to do.

After our parents knew, we finally decided what we would do about our situation. Lee was committed to me, and he said that he would always be there for me if we had the baby and he would support me if we didn't. He made sure that I knew that he was going to be around for "the long haul" no matter what we decided. The next day I made an appointment to have an abortion.

Then it was my turn to talk to his mom. She called me into their living room, and we sat face to face. She told me first how much God loved me, then how much He loved the baby that was growing within me. She then proceeded to explain to me that she had been pregnant with Lee at age 18, and that the Lord had made a way for them. She explained that God always provided what was needed, and although they had sometimes fallen on hard times, Lee never went without anything he truly needed.

She encouraged me and allowed me to hear her story so that I could imagine how my future could go. We sat in that living room for seven hours. I shared my fears, and she promised me that she would help me in any way that she could. Finally, she said, the choice was mine.

When I woke up the next morning, I knew something had changed. I had heard about God's love for my unborn child and I had witnessed a woman who actually walked the path before me. Therefore, I canceled my appointment for the abortion. Although I didn't know the Lord, He knew me, and He loved me through her.

Throughout my pregnancy, Lee and I had our problems. Aside from being very young, neither of us was prepared for the life experiences we were embarking on. Our relationship that had been built on partying and "having fun" together turned into a real chore. He didn't seem to be as committed to growing into the responsible parent that I had expected him to be, and I was worn out by my new life.

Eventually, Lee moved out when our son, Nolan, was only 5 months old. He has had very little involvement with our son since then and has lived a completely separate life from us. He is still flirting with the dangers involved in the lifestyle I left behind.

I gave my life to the Lord when Nolan was 2 years old. I went to a community college during the day and took night classes in order to get my degree. God has made a way for us, and Nolan has never gone without anything he needs. The Lord's provisions are unlimited, and I have witnessed His hand in my life time and time again.

After about five years of being a Christian, I turned my back on the Lord. I met a guy who thought we were soul mates. Instead of praying it through, I trusted him more than I trusted God. I ignored all the warnings the Holy Spirit had stirred up within me.

I ended up getting pregnant and having an abortion. That is an experience I will never forget. I know now that this detour hurtled me directly into the pit that satan had dug for me. He knew my weakness, and I was distracted by the bait he had placed in front of me.

The actual act of going to the clinic and filling out the paperwork seems surreal to me now. I believe it was because of my backsliding and my disconnection with my Savior that I was able to endure the process at all.

The procedure itself was very clinical. I remember that when they "put me under," I was still suffering through the agony of being torn up over my decision until the doctor and nurse had me count backward. Then my mind went blank.

I don't doubt that the tears I shed then were but a small amount as compared to those that were shed in Heaven. All the abortions that went on that day did not go uncounted in Heaven. I am still disturbed and haunted by my decision, but I am forever thankful for God's grace. He knows all my sins, and He forgave me, and, what's more, He still loves me.

I am now left with my thoughts. I wonder if my only son was meant to be a big brother. Who was I to deny him that role in his life? Also, I think about God's ultimate plan for my own life and how I have altered it as a consequence of my sin. I will have the answers to these questions and many others on the Day of Judgment. Until then, I am left to a life in this world, a life of learning and obeying the Lord, as the Spirit leads me.

"Teach me your way, O Lord; lead me in a straight path" (Psalm 27:11).

My body is not my own, yet I have so freely given it away. I know the Lord has forgiven me, and I continue to forgive myself. His plan is to prosper us, and He will use all things for His glory. I believe these truths, and I will share my story with anyone who might be helped by it. Many young girls find themselves in circumstances similar to mine, but the Lord has brought me through those things, and now He can love them through me.

I am a sinner and a mother. Jesus Christ is my Husband, and He is the "Abba Daddy" of my son, Nolan (who is a treasure and a joy). I have prayed that Christ-like characteristics will be developed in Nolan, and I believe the Lord has heard those prayers, for He has given me a wonderful, caring, and generous young boy. It is my honor to be his mom.

Raising my son has not been easy, however, and I mess up quite a bit. But, because of my heavenly Father's forgiveness and mercy, I am able to experience His gifts and blessings in my life every day. I look at my son's face, and realize that he is the miracle of God's love for me during a most desperate time. Although I once turned away from God's love, He waited with open arms for me to come back to Him.

My earthly dad was right when he told me I would never be alone, for I have never been alone and my future has not been what I had planned. However, this was not because of my pregnancy, but because of my new life in Christ. *Praise God!*

Never will I leave you; never will I forsake you (Hebrews 13:5).

Be strong and courageous. Do not be afraid or terrified because of them, for the Lord your God goes with you; he will never leave you nor forsake you (Deuteronomy 31:6).

18

Stories of Two Grandmothers

WHICH ONE ARE YOU?

As I proudly look at my beautiful 22-year-old granddaughter it seems just like yesterday when we all went through the drama surrounding the time when we learned she would be coming to us. I remember that sad, stormy night when my son had come over to our home with his girlfriend and announced that she was pregnant. Both of them did not want to destroy the baby that was forming within her. They had called me frantically, and how I thank God that they came to me for wisdom and love.

The next day my son's girlfriend's mother angrily called me and demanded that her daughter have an abortion. She said that if her daughter did not have an abortion, she would kick her out of the house! She believed her daughter was too young to have a baby and be saddled with the responsibility of motherhood at the tender age of 16.

This distraught woman tried to explain to me that she knew that two wrongs don't make things right, but she believed that abortion would be the right thing to do in this particular situation. Sometimes I wondered if it was a selfish thought on her part. Was her mother thinking of all the heavy responsibilities that would be placed on her if her daughter had a baby? Having raised four children on her own, she didn't want or need the extra burden of another mouth to feed; her life had been one of hardship in that her ex-husband was an alcoholic who used to beat her. Fearing all the possible ramifications of her daughter's pregnancy, she thought it would be best for all concerned if her daughter were to have an abortion.

When my son and his girlfriend broke the news to me, tears started streaming down my face. They told me how much they loved each other and how scared they were of the future. After we all cried together, I invited her to come and live with us, which she agreed to do. Eventually, they got married, and, yes, it was difficult and tough for all of us, but with enough love and support surrounding them, we all made it through.

It was so painful for me to see the lack of understanding that a parent could have toward their child who was crying out for help. She was a child who needed answers and solutions to a difficult problem that she and my son were facing, but instead of receiving help and compassion, they were faced with indifference, a lack of tolerance, and an unwillingness to help in their time of great need. It breaks my heart to know that so many mothers and fathers lack the understanding, compassion, wisdom, and love that their children need to help them get through such difficult times.

This is one of the reasons I have become so active in the pro-life movement. I believe that each conception is the beginning of a new life, and life is so precious and special that we do not have a right to destroy what God has created. Babies truly are miracles from God!

To think that I might have missed out on all the joys and love that my precious granddaughter has given to me if I had given in to the whims of the other grandmother is very upsetting.

My son and daughter-in-law always wanted a large family, but for some reason she was unable to conceive again. How tragic it would have been if my daughter-in-law had caved in to her mother's demand, for she and my son would never have had the opportunity again to become parents. I thank God daily for their *right* choice of keeping their beautiful baby. Today they are now the proud grandparents of my great-grandson, Sebastian!

As Paul said, all things do work together for good in God's plan, if we just accept His precious gift of life! (See Romans 8:28.)

Since she was born, my beautiful granddaughter has had a wonderful relationship with her maternal grandmother. Once her grandmother laid her eyes upon her and held her tenderly in her arms, she realized how joyous and precious this wonderful gift of life is.

Cherish and treasure the gift of life. We only have one chance to do it right!

Love,

CAROLINA CASTORENA

19

In *His* Grip, the Lord Will Keep You

MICHELE'S STORY

Hi! My name is Michele. I am both a birth mother and a mother.

I grew up in a U.S. Navy family with my older sister, my mom, and my dad. My dad was an alcoholic, and he used drugs on and off. His alcoholism landed him in a lot of trouble, but somehow my parents managed to stay together. This was something I did not really appreciate until I began thinking about what it meant to be a parent.

It was 1993. I had just moved back into my parent's house after living on my own with a couple of college friends. I was 23 years old and searching for "what I wanted in life." I had a boyfriend, Chad, and I was trying to figure out where my relationship with him was headed. Something was stirring inside of me to look for more meaning in my life, to look for a change, or something. I couldn't quite put my finger on it exactly, but I was neither content nor satisfied.

For a couple of months I felt numb with regard to my relationship with Chad. While at work one day, I remember thinking, "Why am I doing this? I don't feel loved, respected, or even cared for." In fact, I felt used, and I thought that Chad was taking advantage of me. I didn't know what to do or how to end things, so I just kept seeing him.

One day my period was late, and my world came crashing in on me! I thought, "Oh, no, not me! Not me! Not me! Not me!" I had known it *could* happen, but like so many others, I never believed it would happen to me!

Chad had left for school just a week before this, and all he knew was that my period was late. He just said, "Oh, you're not pregnant." What a help he was!

Well, I took a pregnancy test, and I couldn't believe the results, so I took another test. The result: *positive!* Yes, indeed, I was pregnant! Not knowing what to do, I ran to my sister after work and fell apart in front of her.

My world was closing in on me. I wanted to die. I really did. As I lay prostrate on my sister's living room floor, I cried and cried. I kept repeating, "What am I going to do?" I couldn't think clearly. So many things were racing through my head. It felt like a dozen people were talking all at the same time and they all had made demands of me! I couldn't concentrate. I was shutting down inside.

Then my sister finally had enough of my hysterics and told me to sit up, stop crying, and talk. She was right. I needed to stop and figure out how to deal with this situation.

I had gone to my sister because I knew I could trust her to keep a secret, if I needed her to do so. The first thing that came to my mind was abortion. If I had an abortion, nobody would have to know that I had gotten pregnant, and I could get rid of "my problem."

But deep down inside I knew something wasn't right about that option. I just knew it was not right. I thought back to an experience I had with my roommate just a few months before.

I had taken my roommate to a clinic for an abortion. In so doing, I thought I was supporting my friend. But there was a storm brewing on the inside of me while I sat in the abortion clinic waiting for her. As I drove her home that day, I felt like a deer staring at headlights, for I was stunned. I was frozen, unable to think. It was as if everything was quiet and nothing was moving.

After I took my roommate home and got her settled, I started off for a visit to New York. It was a four-hour drive and there was plenty of time for me to think. Why was I so bothered? Why did I feel so weird? I began to realize that my friend's abortion was troubling me. *What do I believe about it?* It sure was bugging me!

Until then, I had just listened to what people had said about abortion and would accept what they thought without much more than a "That sounds good." I had believed what they told me: "It's a personal decision. You can't tell someone else what to do, and, besides, how could anyone say what they would do unless they had to face it themselves?"

Well, that day I had come as close to experiencing an unplanned pregnancy as I could, without actually being pregnant! As I continued to drive, I felt as if I were drowning in a sea of silence. What was going on? I protested, *I didn't do anything!* Yet, I was haunted by what had happened that day and it rendered me numb. The thought of my friend's abortion was maddening to me, and I kept thinking, *Hey, I wasn't the one who had the abortion! Why am I feeling guilty?*

Then it came to me; it was true guilt that I was experiencing that evening.

I reasoned, *What? Why should I feel guilty!* I refused to accept personal ownership of the guilt and pushed it away, as I made my way to my sister's home in New York. That Sunday I went to church with my mom; this had become my routine when I went home for visits. While in church that morning, I heard a baby crying just a couple of seats away. The baby's cry rang in my ears as if there was a message in the crying that I needed to hear. I couldn't focus on anything but the crying even long after the mother had left with her baby.

Then as if a dam had burst, tears began to flow from my eyes. The more I tried to push back the strong current of tears, the heavier they flowed. I didn't understand how I could feel such sorrow for an abortion that someone else had experienced. Then, suddenly, it felt like the wind had been knocked out of me when I realized for the first time that abortion was death! There had been a death. I had not simply escorted my friend to an abortion clinic; I had taken part in a baby's death! On that fateful day "the problem" had not been taken care of; instead, a life had been snuffed out!

This vivid memory began to fade as I continued to lie on my sister's floor in a daze. I remembered that the experience with my friend had changed my thinking about abortion, and now I knew that abortion ends a life, an innocent life.

I was the one who made the choices that led to an unplanned pregnancy. I am without excuse, and this was *my* problem, not the baby's. Now I have another life to consider, not just my own. Help! I felt like I would rather die than be responsible for another life. I knew I had made a mess out of my own life. How could I handle someone else's? I felt trapped, and there didn't seem to be any way to get out of this responsibility for another life. I realized that a new life had already begun within me, and I would have to answer for whatever decision I would make.

My thoughts then drifted to God. I thought about what I was learning in church. I thought about how much God loves me and how He wants me to give my life to Him. I prayed, "God, do you really want my life? Will you really forgive the wrongs I have done? I am a mess, and I have done some pretty bad things. Just let me die. I am not worth the trouble."

But it was as if I was "double-dog daring" Him. I continued to pray: "OK, God, you want this mess—you got it. I am done with living life on my own terms and making bad choices. So, you got me. Now what?"

After what seemed like a lifetime had passed, I got up off the floor, and my sister and I began to go over my choices. I knew that the first choice I had to make was to choose life or death. I had to decide if I was going to give my baby a chance to live or if I would put an end to the new life within me.

I chose life!

Once I had made this decision, I knew I still had more choices: parenting or adoption?

I felt I was fairly familiar with the choice of parenting, but I wasn't very familiar with adoption. The only thing I knew was that it was an option.

Later that day I broke the news to my mother. Then, once I had confirmed the pregnancy and there were no doubts about it at all, I told the news to Chad, my boyfriend. It was scary to do so, because I wasn't sure what he would do or say, but I was prepared for a variety of responses, and I was ready to stand firm in my decision no matter what he said.

By the time I told Chad, I had already been looking into adoption. I told him I was gathering information and looking at my options, and adoption was a consideration. He surprised me by being very understanding. He said, "I will support you in this."

I was relieved that he didn't have any definite thoughts or ideas about our situation. I was free to look at things on my own. I didn't want to be controlled by anyone. Even though I had felt like a failure with my own life up to this point, I was determined not to fail my child.

I began calling adoption agencies and any groups that had to do with crisis pregnancy. I looked at private adoption and what would be involved with that option. I met with a mother who had adopted a child, and I sought counseling for myself. I wanted to be sure I checked out every possible aspect of adoption.

In the meantime, Chad continued in school, and I was becoming more aware that our relationship did not have a solid foundation. Something was changing within me, and I wanted something different for my life. I found myself hanging out more and more with a new friend who was a Christian. She had something I wanted, a personal relationship with Jesus. Her life showed me that He was real, and she talked to Him like a regular person. As she prayed, she never used fancy words or forms.

For the first time in my life, I saw someone who was *real*. She didn't pretend she had it all together. Some days she would be a "wreck" from the problems of her life, but then she would "unload" on God and get up and move on.

Wow, I thought, *how does she do that?* I wanted what she had, so I started reading my Bible. My friend and I would go to church services, concerts, and all kinds of "God things" together. I was amazed. God was real! I was discovering what I had been looking for all along.

The silent prayer I uttered on that fateful day has changed things completely.

I no longer felt empty. God did care. He did love me, and He has forgiven me!

I was set free from all the guilt I carried from the past. I not only began to see hope in the future, but I wanted a future! I wasn't alone anymore and I knew it. I felt like there was a colorful garden of sweet flowers blooming and filling the empty, colorless spaces inside of me.

Despite all this, though, I still had troubles and problems to deal with. I was still pregnant, and I still had to make a decision! I lost my job and spent many days home alone at my parents' house. I used this time to search out different adoption agencies, ask many questions, read books, and pray for the right things to do. I cried many tears over this decision.

In the beginning I was more concerned with how being pregnant affected me. I was in no way ready to be a mother, and I did I not really want to be one. I knew what single moms had to deal with, and I knew I did *not* want that kind of life.

Then my focus underwent a radical change. What about the baby? What kind of life will the baby have? Did I want my child to go through the heartaches I went through? My childhood was very rough. I admit things could have been worse, but I wanted something better for my baby.

A good parent wants a life for their child that is better than theirs was. I thought about the life we would have if I parented my baby instead of going the adoption route. I would be a single mom, and Chad might be involved *maybe* on weekends. I knew that a child needs consistency and parents who are available. I would have to work many hours to provide for our needs and pay for daycare.

I thought about how I would try to teach my child the values I believed in, values that Chad most likely would disagree with. He might even teach the opposite to the baby. Moreover, I couldn't count on Chad and I being together, for we were already going our separate ways. I was changing, and I wanted different things in my life. Chad and I didn't share much in common anymore. I knew that, even if we tried to make it work, we would eventually split up. I wasn't about to allow myself to think that somehow "love" would get us through and we would live happily ever after, having all the things we dreamed of; they call this type of thinking a fairy tale for a reason!

I wanted my child to start off right. I wanted the baby to have a stable family with two parents who were ready and waiting to be parents. I wanted my child to have a life without the troubles I had gone through, and I wanted him/her to have more opportunities than I had when I was growing up.

I wanted more for the baby than I could provide. I tried to be realistic about everything. I knew I could not provide what I desired for my child, not on my own anyway. I began to realize that through adoption I *could* provide all the things I wanted for the baby and give myself another chance to make something of my life.

After much prayer and tears, I began to work with an agency that I felt comfortable with. They helped me think through the decision in great detail. I went over the pros and cons of adoption and parenting, and I was able to talk it over with someone who was objective. I was not alone in this decision at all. I learned I had a great deal of control in the process. I could choose and meet the parents, have contact with them after the adoption, and plan out the birthing experience. There was much more openness to adoption than there used to be.

I began to prepare an adoption plan for my child. My prayers were answered in great detail, giving me the assurance I needed to keep going. I kept Chad "in the loop" at all times, telling him of my concerns, thoughts, and plans. He was supportive and even met with my counselor and me. We began to make decisions together. We talked about what we would hope the adoptive parents would be like, and we looked at couples together. How different we were really came clear as we went through this process together! I would look at the couple's faith and values, while Chad would look at what sports the husband played. Sometimes I would get so mad at him! I thought he wasn't being serious enough, but I was determined to accept Chad's input and be thankful that he was being supportive.

As the months went by, I felt like I could become a case study at a mental institution. I went through so many different emotions and fears! Many times I would think, *What if my baby hates me for this?* or *What if he* or *she doesn't understand why I am doing this?* Then I would be overwhelmed with guilt for feeling that I was being very selfish for placing my child in adoption even though people would say to me, "You are so selfless to make this choice. I admire you."

I would think, *What, are you kidding me? You don't know how selfish I am. I don't want to be a mom. I am thinking of my own life. I am a terrible person!*

At each confusing crossroad, I would write out what I was thinking and feeling and share my thoughts and feelings with God and my counselor. Then, somehow, in the same way that mud settles to the bottom of a puddle, I could see clearly and sift through my emotions and deal with them one at a time.

Eventually the guilt I felt was lifted. I had an inner assurance that it was all right for me to think of my own needs and to be happy that I would get a second chance.

I also realized I was afraid of letting go. I had been going through the motions of all the planning while not letting myself get attached to the baby. I was afraid of bonding with the baby, and I was terrified of the sorrow I would feel when the baby was born. The truth was that I enjoyed feeling the baby move inside of me. I wanted to choose a special name for him/her, a name with a meaning that would reflect how much I loved this baby. I was excited as I thought about what the baby would look like. Would the baby have hair at birth, and what color would it be? Would the baby look like me or more like Chad?

One haunting question remained: How would I handle having to say goodbye to my baby? As I talked things through with my counselor, I learned it was healthy for me to love and bond with the baby. I then coined the phrase: "You have to say hello before you can say goodbye."

Next, I began to plan for my time in the hospital. I knew I wouldn't have much time, but I had decided I wanted to have my baby with me as much as I could, and I wanted to get lots of pictures and memories.

Finally, the time to meet the couple Chad and I had agreed on arrived. I had been certain for a while that they were "the ones," and I was eager to meet them. Chad, on the other hand, did not want to meet them. He wouldn't accept anyone's help in this process and wanted to deal with things on his own. I felt bad for him. He was missing out on a lot, but I continued on.

My mom went with me to meet the couple. It was awkward at first, but as soon as we got the initial hellos over with and began talking, we were very much at ease with one another. I was so impressed by their expression of love and concern for *me* during our visit! I hadn't been expecting that. I thought all the talk would be about the baby, and rightly so! But they showed me that they also wanted to know about the mother of the child that they would be taking home one day.

They asked what interests and hobbies I had and if there was anything I did that was particularly unique or special to me. They wanted to know even the small details of my life, and I could quickly tell that they really cared. They asked me to share as much personal information that I felt comfortable about sharing, because they wanted to eventually pass it along to the baby. I discovered we had a lot in common, and I felt that, if we had met under different circumstances, we definitely would have been friends. I was amazed by this, and I knew in my heart that this couple would be the right parents for my baby.

I left that meeting feeling as if I had just visited with angels, and I believed God was watching over the adoption with great detail and interest.

I began collecting special things for a basket that I would send home with the baby. I included things I bought as well as things that were special to me: a cookie recipe for which I won a blue ribbon at the local 4-H Fair, a cassette of special songs I grew up with, pictures of my family, a baseball cap from Chad and a couple of pictures of Chad, too. I had written out Psalm 121, framed it, and lovingly put this Scripture that had helped to sustain me into the basket.

I also planned to write a letter to the baby and the parents. There was so much I wanted to tell them, and in a letter I could be sure it would be said just in case anything would happen that would prevent us from ever meeting again. Meeting again was a deep longing of my heart, one that I would trust God for. I learned to place the deep things of my heart in God's care and trust that He would take care of my baby and my future.

At last I had peace in the depths of my soul. I carried this peace right through the birth of my baby to the placing of him in the couple's arms just before they took him home. We planned to correspond with one another through the coming years. In this way I would know about my son and how he was doing. I would not be left guessing about him and his welfare through the years of his development into manhood. I was so happy to know that we would remain in contact, and I planned to write letters to them, as well, in which I would share my life with him and his family.

Though I shed many tears during the time I spent in the hospital, I did not regret a thing. Oh, I knew my pain and sorrow would be great, but a mother's love looks beyond her pain to do what is best for her child. I determined that I would not focus on *myself*, but on the wonderful life that was in store for my son.

Yes, *my* son. I had a boy, and I named him Samuel. He was born with beautiful dark hair, olive skin, and dark brown eyes. My mom told me that Samuel looked just like I did when I was born. I cherished every moment I had with him. Each and every day of my life I hold Samuel deep within my heart.

During this time some people believed that I didn't know what I was doing and that I had made a mistake by choosing adoption, but a mother knows, and this mother has a peace that passes all understanding.

Adoption Is a Loving Choice

Since that time, I have gone on to intern in a ministry that helps troubled men and women. The Lord has put a desire within my heart to comfort others with the comfort I myself have received. I have sought to become a voice for the "adoption option," and I hope to educate people about adoption. I have found that there is a great misunderstanding concerning adoption both within the church and the secular community.

While I was engaged in this ministry, I met the man who became my husband, and we have been married for ten years. We have three beautiful children (Josiah, Jedidiah, and Trinity), and another one is on the way! I continue to receive updates about my son Samuel; he is 12 years old as I write this. God has been so good to us through the years, and it is because of His Son that I have this story to share with you.

> I lift up my eyes to the hills—where does my help come from? My help comes from the Lord, the Maker of heaven and earth. He will not let your foot slip—he who watches over you will not slumber; indeed, he who watches over

Israel will neither slumber nor sleep. The Lord watches over you—the Lord is your shade at your right hand: the sun will not harm you by day, nor the moon by night. The Lord will keep you from all harm—he will watch over your life; the Lord will watch over your coming and going both now and forevermore (Psalm 121).

20
Precious Gifts of Life and Love

CINDY'S STORY

The phone rang. "Hello, Cindy? This is Marian." Wow, I hadn't heard from Marian for 15 years! Her father had died when she was a young child, and while I was in college, her mother passed away. My mother had kept in contact with her all of these years, helping her whenever she could. So I thought, why would she be calling me?

"Marian, it is so good to hear your voice. It has been ages since I last saw you. How are you?"

"I've been great. I've gotten married since I last talked to you, and life is good. I have some exciting news to share with you. I have been working as a midwife in a hospital in Nevada, and one of my patients asked me if I knew of anyone who would be a good parent. I immediately thought of you. Cindy. How would you like to adopt a baby?"

My heart stood still. I couldn't believe my ears, and I excitedly responded, "Of course, Marian, we would be thrilled. What do we have to do?"

"I can't give you any details right now, but you will need to have your attorney call me, and I will put them in contact with the birth mother."

She thought of *me*? Wow! My husband and I had been praying for a child for eight years. We had gone to a fertility clinic and I had even tried being inseminated twice, but it was all to no avail. Then our doctor died in a horrible plane crash, so we gave up when we discovered that we would have to start the testings all over again with a new doctor.

We had eight weeks to put it all together. We had to deal with attorneys in Nevada and California, plus various social workers. What if we did all of this and the mother would change her mind? Was the baby a boy or a girl? What race was the baby? Is the baby healthy?

So many questions raced through our minds, but these were questions that would have to remain unanswered for now. My husband and I talked it over and decided we had to take the chance. What we did know was that we really wanted this baby.

As we learned later, the mother was seven months pregnant when she went into premature labor. Marian was her nurse when she arrived at the hospital to stop the delivery. As they chatted, Marian learned that the mother had been engaged to the baby's father when she had become pregnant. Her fiancé got "cold feet," and then he then abandoned her and encouraged her to have an abortion.

In her mind, it seemed like the logical thing to do, since she was working at Burger King and had no other means of supporting herself, much less a child. But in her heart she knew she couldn't have an abortion. She realized it wasn't right to destroy her baby. She loved this baby that was growing within her, and, although she could not support him and give him much, she could at least give life to her baby boy.

She told Marian that she had been thinking of giving the baby up for adoption, but she didn't know how to go about doing that. Marian had responded to her, "You must really love this child to be so concerned about his welfare and not consider your own."

The mother responded, "You are the first person I have met who really understands. Most people think I want to abandon him, which is not true. I want to give him everything, but I have so little to offer him."

As it turns out, our precious David was born July 24, 1993. In the hospital the birth parents came into the room while Marian was holding

David. The mother looked down at him, patted his tiny head, turned to me and commented, "I do good work, don't I?"

I exclaimed, "Yes, you do. He is absolutely beautiful!" I praise God every day for the love of a mother who would carry her child for nine months and then give it up for adoption. So many young girls and ladies would rather take the easy way out and abort the child.

I have had many conversations over the years with David's birth mother, and we send her pictures regularly. She still loves him with all of her heart. Their separation is still very painful for her, but she knows that what she did was a good thing. That fact helps to ease her pain. She realizes and knows that he is in a good and loving home with a mother and father who love and want him very much. He is safe, secure, happy and he is doing great.

When David was 1 year old, I became pregnant. My world was magical, and I now felt complete. After all of these years, I would soon have two beautiful children to love, cherish, and adore.

I was 36 at the time of my pregnancy. Because of my age, my primary care doctor recommended that I undergo some tests to verify if the baby would be healthy. He said, "There is the possibility of Downs syndrome and other possible problems due to your age."

He continued, "If it turns out that your child has any of these problems, you will then have the option of aborting the child before your pregnancy gets too far along."

I explained to him that I do not believe in abortion. I also said that I did not want to do anything that would place my baby at risk. Therefore, I turned down all of the tests and trusted God for the results.

My pregnancy was going along fine, and I felt life inside of me. My doctor sent me in for the sonogram at five months. The technician showed me the baby's heartbeat. This worker had been rather quiet most of the time and had seemed somewhat preoccupied. I tried to be friendly and chatty, but she would only answer a few of my questions. She tried to get all of the requested pictures, but there was very little cooperation from my little baby boy.

At seven months, my doctor sent me to a specialist for high-risk pregnancies because of my age. Since everything seemed to be going well, I drove myself to his office. The technician doing the sonogram excused herself to find the doctor.

When the doctor came in, he informed me that there were problems with my baby. He explained to us that the baby's organs had not developed correctly. He went on, "He has a cleft pallet, and the center of his brain is missing. Your child has Chromosome 13 Syndrome, and he will die once we deliver him."

This doctor was very irritated when he found out that I was seven months pregnant and did not know the condition of my child. He then called my husband who was at his work and informed him of the condition of our son. He asked if he would please come to the office as soon as possible.

When my husband arrived, the specialist proceeded to call my doctor while we sat in the room and listened, and he berated my doctor for not informing us of the baby's problems sooner. "Yes, the Walkers are here with me....Yes we can have this conversation later."

As it turns out, our doctor had suspected problems after he saw the first sonogram. It showed that the center of the baby's brain was not developed. But, because he knew about my position on abortion, he was just giving me clues that there might be something wrong with our baby. He was also allowing me to get further along before dropping this bombshell on my hopes and dreams.

I carried my little baby boy for two more months, and during this time I had to make funeral arrangements for him. It was very difficult when people would come up to me and congratulate me in anticipation of the upcoming birth. They were very excited about the life inside of me, not knowing that he would not live long after his birth. Their intentions were good and kind, and most of the time I was able to smile at them and say thank you for their kind words, but occasionally the truth was too much, and I would tell them that the child would not live.

My sadness grew as I would try to convince myself that maybe the doctors were wrong, that possibly my little boy was really perfect. He would kick and move inside of me, and I loved him like I had loved no one else. I cried, because I wanted to give him everything, anything, but I could give him nothing except my love and tears.

After all was done and finished, and our baby Isaac was laid in the ground, sadness and sorrow began to sweep over me. But then I would hear, "Mommy! Mom! Mom!"

God knew my pain in advance, so He had provided for me a beautiful little miracle named David who was now 2 years old, and he was so precious and so full of love. I cherish, treasure, and love our boy.

Someone might ask me: "If you had the chance to make your choices all over again, would you change your decision about aborting your son after finding out about his condition?"

My answer is an unequivocal no! I would not have changed a thing. Isaac was my one-minute miracle, and I was going to give him life for as long as I could, even if it was only for one minute. His life growing inside of me was far too precious to destroy.

21

If I Knew Then What I Know Now

THE REST OF CHERYL'S STORY

As they say, hindsight is always 20-20. Too bad it always comes too late. We become so much wiser and have more understanding of our life journey and issues when we are able to look back and reflect upon our lives. However, isn't it sad that we didn't know back then, what we know now?

A lot of us live in the terror and fear of rejection that will occur when we announce to others that the precious gift of life is growing within us. We tend to fear what other people will think and do if they discover or learn the truth of where we've been or what we have done. So we try to cover up our mistakes, which in turn cause us to make even more wrong choices, then only to discover later in life that the reactions and responses of others would have been totally different than we thought they would be. We are usually surprised to learn this.

It was Mother's Day 1992 when I shared for the first time with my parents about the abortion that had happened 17 years before. They had come down from Sacramento to visit for the week. We were all in the kitchen as mom was preparing lunch for dad and me. We started to reminisce about the past, both the good times and the bad, including my relationship with my ex-husband. All of a sudden, without forethought, I shared the facts about my abortion with my parents and told them how it had destroyed our marriage relationship. The room became silent as my parents were taking in my words. Their eyes were so sad.

My mother remained silent for the longest time, then she said quietly, "Now I understand why your mother-in-law wanted to move up the wedding date. But I told her we couldn't because you had to finish school first. To have a wedding during the school term would be too difficult on everybody. Now I understand why she wanted you to get married sooner. She must have known about the baby."

Being Chinese, my mother-in-law understood the Chinese culture. She knew that I would be disowned for shaming and disgracing my parents. So she didn't press it any further when my parents said no.

My father didn't say a word. After hearing all this, he started to weep. He left the kitchen and went into the family room over to the game table where he sat down and laid his head upon the table and cried. As I walked over to him, I began to cry, as well. As I got closer to dad, he began to sob loudly. I put my arms around him and said, "Don't cry, daddy, I am so sorry for what I did."

Sobbingly he replied, "No, Cheryl. I am so sorry. Can you forgive me for being so strict with you as you were growing up? If you weren't so scared to come to me, you would have had the baby, and we would have accepted and loved our grandchild. Please forgive me for making you go through that ordeal. Now I understand why you changed after you got married. You became so distant to us and I thought that we had lost our little girl. Please forgive me!"

I had only seen my father cry twice in my entire life. Once was when his mother died 15 years earlier and the second time was when I shared about my abortion—the death of his first grandchild. Dad was grieving over the lost relationship with his daughter and his aborted grandchild.

Sadly, as I looked back upon my life, I realized that I had reacted out of fear, which was easy for me to do. When you don't have all the correct information at hand to help you decide and choose properly, you end up making wrong choices. I was given incorrect information while I was growing up.

When you know that breaking the rules and regulations will cause you to suffer the penalty of being disowned, you believe it. You believe it when you hear the threat, "If you get pregnant before you get married or bring disgrace or shame to your parents, you will be disowned." Hearing this all your life, both as a child growing up and throughout your teens, you tend to believe it as truth. I didn't realize that my father's bark had no bite to it, and that despite whatever I did, my father would always love me. Unfortunately, I found this out too late. Dad had put down the rules of life so that we would fear him and keep within the confines of good moral behavior. He knew that boundaries and good behavior would keep us out of harm's way and our lives would be safe from heartaches and danger.

Bringing out the truth of my sins to my parents actually brought a healing to them and to me, and it gave them a more complete understanding of why their little girl had changed from one who used to be so loving and happy to one who was so distant, lonely, and sad.

On that fateful day my mother and father knew I had never stopped loving them. They also realized that it was my sin that had caused the separation in our relationship. If I had my life to live over again, I would trust in the love of my parents to help me, to love me, to forgive me, and to stand by me.

I pray that my four children will always know there is nothing that could ever cause my love for them to cease. No matter what happens in their lives, they will always be able to come and talk with me.

I will not judge them, and I will always love them and help them.

Love is patient, love is kind. It does not envy, it does not boast, it is not proud. It is not rude, it is not self-seeking, it is not easily angered, it keeps no record of wrongs. Love does not delight in evil but rejoices with the truth. It always protects, always trusts, always hopes, always perseveres. Love never fails (1 Corinthians 13:4-8).

May my child never have to cry out: *"Do not reject me or forsake me, O God my Savior. Though my mother and my father forsake me, the Lord will receive me"* (Ps. 27:9-10).

We, as parents, must never forsake our children and the future generations that come from the wombs of our children. We need to be like God who tells us that He will never forsake us.

The following prayer is for parents who did not stand by their children during their times of crisis—times when they needed loving, caring, understanding, and guidance. Due to their lack of correct guidance, they influenced their children to make wrong decisions regarding abortion and life. In so doing, they caused both parent and child to suffer severe mental anguish and remorse that could continue for the rest of their lives.

A Parent's Prayer

Heavenly Father, please forgive me for forsaking my child during his/her time of need when he/she needed me the most. Please forgive me for my wrong decisions, thoughts, choices, attitude, anger, lack of understanding, and lack of love for him/her during the time of crisis. Please heal me and my family and restore us.

Thank you for forgiving me and helping us. Give me the wisdom and strength to handle things correctly. Help me to forgive my child and the person that they were involved with. Give me the compassion and the understanding for my child that you so graciously and lovingly give to me, so we can work through our situation in the best possible way. Amen.

22

Stand With Us

Around the world, there were over 46 million abortions conducted in the year 2004. Twenty million of these were obtained illegally.

There are approximately 126,000 abortions conducted each day. This means that with every blink of your eyes, someone is having an abortion.

There have been more babies killed in one year than the number of American soldiers (approximately 1.19 million) who have been killed during all the wars the United States has been involved in from the 1800s until today.

In the year 2004 there were approximately 1.37 million abortions performed in the United States.

These statistics are frightening, disturbing, and alarming. We have literally committed genocide against two generations of children who would have been our world's future wealth and heritage.

Forty-three percent of the women in the United States under the age of 45 have experienced an abortion. These statistics do not include the number of men who have helped to make this decision or stood silently by while the women made their choices.

Abortion is no respecter of any age group, race, culture, economic condition, gender, intelligence, occupation, city, neighborhood, or lifestyle. Abortion has become an epidemic of choice that crosses all lines of life, situations, and style of life. It is affecting the world today and causing people who have made this choice to go underground with their personal thoughts and secret sins, living lives of silent pain, anguish, and regret.

If you look around, you will see us everywhere. We are the living dead caught up in the coffin of our choice. Some of us appear to be well-adjusted and functional, but we are hurting deep down inside where no one can see our pain. There are a lot of us who are so out of control trying to escape the pain that we become non-functional and drop out of society. As we do so, we are nailing the lids of our coffins shut and pounding them down with our anger, our self–destructive and addictive behaviors, and our guilt. This keeps us from living life completely.

Many of us who have made the abortion choice are so ashamed of our decision that we lie shipwrecked in our thought life, and our lives become like tombs, prisons of guilt, shame, self-condemnation, and fear. We fear what other people will think of us, or what they will do to us once they find out about our mistake. But most of all, we fear our eternal destination of damnation when we die, for deep down in our hearts we know that there is a God out there who judges sin. Yes, we are the walking dead.

That is why "the silent minority" needs to come forth. By "silent minority" I mean those who have experienced abortion or who have been part of someone's choice to have an abortion and have heard, received, and accepted the good news of Jesus. These are the ones who need to stand up. They need to testify of the loving kindness of God's grace, mercy, and forgiveness to those who are hurting as a result of their choices and decisions. In so doing, they will help those who are hurting unlock their prison doors, open up their coffins, and come back from the living dead to living life again.

We have to remember, life is not just about you and only you, but life is all about those closest to us—our family, our friends, our co-workers, our acquaintances, our neighborhood, our work environment, our church, our city, our country, our world. We need to reach out and help all of our brothers and sisters who are suffering as a result of bad choices in their lives and help them to overcome their silent anguish.

We need to talk. We need to speak out to reach a generation that does not understand the full consequences of abortion and the purpose of life. This younger generation has been raised up to believe that there are no boundaries in life and that anything goes. Some even believe that abortion is a form of birth control and a quick solution to a mistake or inconvenience. They are taught that a fetus is just a blob of tissue and not a living being. These misconceptions need to be replaced with the real truth, that God has created mankind for a purpose. With every conception, God creates a potential being for a specific purpose. Creation is not an accident, but it is predestined and purposed by God.

So there we are, the silent minority, and one day we may become the silent majority, if we refuse to tell of God's forgiveness, redeeming grace, and purpose for life. We are everywhere. We could be the salesperson who helps you, the bank teller, your teacher, your friend, your classmate, your co-worker, your Sunday school teacher, your doctor, your lawyer, your gardener, your babysitter, your mother, your aunt, your grandmother, your sister, your brother, your father, your uncle, your grandfather, your cousin, your child. We truly are everywhere.

There is no class, job, or career classification, level of education, race, culture, or age difference that singles us out specifically. We are the walking wounded of a decision that was not well thought out. Our decision to have an abortion was made out of fear and ignorance of all the consequences that would come forth from this one choice. Some of us were forced into making this decision by a second or a third party, or by someone who had authority over us.

Unfortunately, there are many of us who did not hear the good news of Jesus and the forgiveness of sin, so we live in the terror, trauma, and darkness of our thoughts, choice, and guilt. We are thinking and believing in our anguished hearts that there is no other way but downwards after we die, and this thought is just the beginning of the agonizing concept of living eternally in hell. In a very real sense, then our hell begins here, on earth.

However, when you get to a point of self-realization and a realization of the Truth, you then know who you are, who you belong to, and who created you and knew you before you were formed or were ever born. You then will realize how greatly loved you are.

> *Before I formed you in the womb I knew you, before you were born I set you apart* (Jeremiah 1:5).

> *"For I know the plans I have for you," declares the Lord, "plans to prosper you and not to harm you, plans to give you hope and a future. Then you will call upon me and come and pray to me, and I will listen to you. You will seek me and find me when you seek me with all your heart. I will be found by you," declares the Lord, "and will bring you back from captivity"* (Jeremiah 29:11).

> *For you created my inmost being; you knit me together in my mother's womb. I praise you because I am fearfully and wonderfully made; your works are wonderful, I know that full well. My frame is not hidden from you when I was made in the secret place. When I was woven together in the depths of the earth, your eyes saw my unformed body. All the days ordained for me were written in your book before one of them came to be. How precious to me are your thoughts, O God!* (Psalm 139:13-17)

> *In his [God's] hand is the life of every creature and the breath of all mankind* (Job 12:10).

> *Behold, children are a heritage from the Lord* (Psalm 127:3 NKJV).

My wonderful friend, Consuelo Peterson, wrote the following song entitled, "For Sure." As you read its inspiring words, you will know that you are greatly loved.

FOR SURE

As sure as the sun comes up every day,
His love for me won't go away.
As sure as the stars light up that dark sky,
His love for me will not die.
As sure as this world goes around and around
My heart to His is ever bound.

As sure as the waves meet that ocean shore,
His love for me is secure,
For sure His love for me will never end
He knew me before my life began.
Lord, you're faithful,
Your love is eternal.
That's for sure, yes, for sure.

As sure as seasons always come and go,
His love for me I'll surely know.
As sure as the rain will fall to the ground,
His loving voice will resound.

© Consul Peterson

Yes, those things are "for sure." God has loved us so much that we have His Word and assurance that He will always love us and forgive us.

For God so loved the world that he gave his one and only Son, that whoever believes in him shall not perish but have eternal life. For God did not send his Son into the world to condemn the world, but to save the world through him. Whoever believes in him is not condemned, but whoever does not believe stands condemned already because he has not believed in the name of God's one and only Son (John 3:16-18).

And the baby says, "Make me your choice. There is an angel standing by you. Listen to my still, small voice calling out your name, 'Mommy, Mommy, Daddy, Daddy.' I'm whispering to you, 'Please make me your choice.'"

23

Post-Abortion Syndrome

Abortion is a losing proposition. There is no easy, safe, or painless abortion, and there is not one winning solution to an abortion, because it causes the violent death of a baby's life. Abortion brings with it severe mental stress, anguish, and emotional and psychological effects that are far beyond what anyone ever anticipates, imagines, or comprehends. These consequences and results of abortion are known as post-abortion syndrome.

The symptoms of post-abortion syndrome are:

1. Anxiety
2. Confusion, disorganization
3. Hopelessness
4. Feelings of tiredness (lethargy)
5. Anger, bitterness
6. Guilt and shame
7. Extreme sadness
8. Recurring thoughts of the abortion or the aborted baby

9. Inability to participate fully in life (Life becomes blocked by numbness and indecision.)

10. Long-term grief reactions

11. Suicidal thoughts

12. Emotional outbursts (anger or tears)

13. Isolation and withdrawal

14. Addictions, drug and/or alcohol dependency

15. Intimacy (sexual and physical) dysfunctions, and difficulty keeping close relationships

16. Nightmares or sleep disorders

17. Migraine headaches

18. Low self-esteem

19. Memory repression

20. Increased alcohol and drug use

21. Compulsions to touch or to avoid babies

If you are experiencing four or more of these symptoms, we suggest that you seek professional and confidential assistance and counseling to help you overcome the effects of this traumatic time in your life.

If you are facing an unplanned pregnancy, you should seek qualified, professional, and confidential assistance to help you make the correct choice. There is really no easy way out, except to keep the precious gift of life within you; for the aftermath of an abortion will cause you severe mental, emotional, physical, and spiritual stress and dysfunction for years to come. Remember, a couple who wants to adopt your baby will lose that beautiful opportunity.

There are wonderful couples who cannot have children of their own, and they may have been waiting a long time to adopt a baby. This couple would love and cherish your child throughout his or her life. Give the gift of life and love. Adoption is a loving choice! There are over 2 million couples in the United States waiting to adopt a newborn baby.

If I had known of all the issues, emotional pain, and consequences I would encounter as a result of that first abortion, I would never have had the abortion. I wish I would have had a strong Christian friend in whom I could have confided. I know that such a friend would have pointed me in the right direction. I wish, also, that I would have had a good, informative book to read, a book that would have warned me about all the negative things related to an abortion.

Unfortunately, however, through my ignorance, I had to learn about the truth the hard way.

My prayer for you is that your choice will be a good choice, the right choice so that you will avoid all the pain I have had to go through. Choose life so all may live fully—you, your baby, and all your loved ones!

Remember, your choice doesn't just affect you—it also affects all those around you.

May God's love help you through this life and death crisis. My prayer for you is that you will allow God into your life and invite Him into your heart so that He can richly bless you with His love, peace, and forgiveness and bring you to wholeness in His strong and loving arms.

24

Coming Out of the Cave

DONELL'S STORY

Sometimes we feel that our lives and our life steps really don't matter in this chaotic world in which we live. However, I have come to realize that our total being, our life story, is very vital to the issues and existence of all mankind. We are here to help one another and to bring those who are in despair and deep trouble to a point of hope and victory in their lives. No matter how foolish, sad, or out of control you may think your life is or has been, you are significant.

You are vital to the very fabric of mankind. Every step you take and every movement you make will have an impact on someone's life. Through your choices and actions you can allow someone in need to overcome any situation that life has thrown at them. These actions are your footprints, and they can bring peace, understanding, forgiveness, and, most of all, love to others. What are the impacts of your life, the footprints that you are making and leaving behind? May they be imprints of love, peace, and forgiveness.

As I was completing this book, I still doubted whether my testimony would affect the lives of others. I feared, as I was coming out of my "cave of hiding" after all these years, what might greet me at the cave entrance once I stepped out into the light.

Would condemnation, judgment, and shame be hurled against me? Or would there be attitudes of disgust, aversion, anger, hatred, or rejection waiting for me?

So many of our fears and thoughts come upon us as we ponder whether we are doing the right thing or not. It seemed so much safer in the dark cave of my life, for there I was isolated and alone and did not have to interact, react, or communicate with anyone. All I had to do was just sit in the dark and exist. I could just "vegetate" while I was there. My life was in a state of "suspended animation." In my cave of darkness I could be numb and lifeless, for I was like a robot—dead, with no thoughts, no feelings, no emotions, no life. Was this any way to live?

No, this is not how God intended our lives to be lived, hidden, hurt, dark and dismal, all alone. We were all made to live life abundantly and fully with our loved ones, our family, our friends, and our world.

During the period when I was reflecting on all this, I received an e-mail from Donell, and it truly blessed my heart. It encouraged me and confirmed that I was doing the right thing by coming out of my cave existence.

When I arrived at the entrance of my cave, I discovered love, compassion, understanding, encouragement, love, strength, hope, and peace. But most of all, I discovered that my heavenly Father and all of my loved ones who had been waiting so long and desperately for my return were there, waiting for me with open arms.

Let me share Donell's e-mail with you.

Hello Cheryl,

Just a note to let you know that you have impacted my life with your vision and your new project. It's a blessing to the world. I know that God is pleased that you are silent no more. I met you at the ITWLA Leadership Conference and we talked about your dream and I bought your book and CDs.

I started to read your book that afternoon on my way home. I could not put it down. When I waited in the car that night for my children at Junior Achievers, I continued to read. It was amazing. It helped me understand so many things.

My aunt once told me that she believed that my mother had an abortion once. Reading your book has helped me to understand the pain she must have felt, because she was a very compassionate woman. I believe now that her abortion was the secret that she had kept hidden, a secret that caused her to be a closet drinker. Thank you so much. The healing process comes with enlightenment.

Also, my dad admitted to abortions that had taken place several years ago, and now I understand why the light seems to be out in him. He seems to feel that he must not enjoy life anymore. He is a very accomplished, professional musician and has lived all over the world. Now he's given his life to the Lord and has returned home. However, he has stopped playing music; it seems that he's lost his love for everything, but everyday he calls me and tells me he loves me, just like my mom used to do. Now I can minister to him because of you.

All the best to you and your family. May the Lord increase you and your children more and more. I also agree with your prayers for your ex-husband. All the best to Lornah. I am happy that she made the right choice.

Blessings, Donell

The following is my response to Donell and our ongoing correspondence with each other.

Dear Donell,

I am so happy that my book ministered to you and gave you a deeper understanding of your parents. The pain and remorse we hide deep within is something no one can fathom.

The song I wrote, "If They Only Knew," expresses the deep feelings I once felt…"if they knew the truth about me, would they still love me, if they knew."

Thank God for His loving grace in our lives. May He bless you and your father richly with His peace and healing, as He heals your wounded spirits. God loves your father greatly, and I truly believe that he will soon receive the joy and passion back into his life, once he understands that he must forgive himself, for God has already done so!

I pray that God will restore to your dad his love for music and that he will once again play so that the world can enjoy his marvelous gift!

Donell, I was wondering if I could use parts of your letter in my book, for I believe it will minister to our brothers and sisters who have experienced what you have felt. I thank you for your beautiful letter.

I look forward to meeting you again in January or February when I come to the Bahamas. Please keep me posted on your dad. May God richly bless you and your family!

God Bless, Cheryl

Hi, Cheryl,

After just discovering the truth about my mother's abortion about two weeks ago, I have mixed feelings at the moment about sharing it, because she had never shared this with anyone. I never told her that I knew. I wanted to preserve her memory. I don't want people to suffer the way she did either. At the end she got her life straight with God and made us promise that we'll see her again. That was her only concern. She was so very special.

However, I believe it will help others to make the right choice. With regards to my dad, he told me about it ten years ago in confidence. I needed counseling after that, so I went to my pastor at the time. She helped me to understand what they (he and his friend for 21 years) were feeling. I was angry and devastated, but she helped me. I came to understand that because God forgives, so could I.

I would like to talk to my father about sharing this part of our story first, and I'll let you know. I'll be spending some time with him in about two weeks. I don't mind you using my name, though. I believe that when he is ready he will share. Who knows? He may be ready now. I'll talk to him. Please be patient with me.

Blessing and Shalom, Donell

Hi Donell!

I believe that once your father forgives himself and all the people involved with the decision (i.e. girlfriend, your mom, the doctor, etc.) and realizes that God has truly forgiven him, his joy will come back. Does your dad know that you have forgiven him and that you love him very much? Sometimes we need to hear the actual words. You might want to share my book with your dad.

You are blessed, Cheryl

Hi Cheryl,

Thanks for your e-mail. I believe that God ordained this time of fellowship for us, and I believe His purpose will prevail. My daughter has an audio report to make on Abortion and Miscarriages for her project. It seems as if abortion is viewed as an unsolvable problem in the world. Among others, her project will be used in discussions to guide national policy. So far she has all the information she needs related to miscarriages.

She has reviewed your book and wants to know whether you'd like to offer a response to abortion. She also wants to use your book as a reference. It has been a pleasure to meet with you. If there is anything I can do to benefit you or assist you in any way, please let me know. Also, you can feel free to use my letters.

Blessings and Shalom, Donell

Good morning, Donell!

It was such a pleasure to talk with you this morning. You continually bless my heart! Your daughter is certainly welcome to use excerpts from my book.

The chapter entitled, "Stand With Us," and the first part of "Post-Abortion Syndrome" deal with how abortion is a losing proposition.

Also, there is Rod Parsley's book on moral clarity *Silent No More*. This is a great book that is impacting America.

I thank you for your prayers. Please continually keep me in prayer that God's perfect will shall continually be done in the ministry that He has called me to do. The book is to be published by Destiny Image in 2006.

May His will be continually performed in our lives, and may the ministry that God has put before you be richly blessed.

Love, Cheryl

Hi, Donell!

Thank you for all that great information. It is very valuable to me! I thank you for your wonderful support, your prayers, and the vision God has revealed to you.

Saying the words "I love you" is truly very powerful! I know that my parents loved me, but as I was growing up and in my adult years they were never able to say the words. This is because they never heard it from their parents.

Fifteen years ago, after a telephone conversation with my mom, I concluded the call with, "I love you, mom." My mother did not know how to respond to my statement and so she laughed. This hurt my heart. I felt hurt because she couldn't say the words since they were so foreign to her. After several more calls that ended with "I love you," my mother was then able to respond to me. At first she would respond with, "Me, too." Then finally one day she was actually able to say, "I love you."

Since my divorce, I have always made it a point to tell my kids that I love them. Now they are adults, and I still tell them that I love them. We all need to know and hear this, for it is a warm, fuzzy feeling that makes you feel so good and special!

I will be in prayer for you and your father. God wants him to be totally set free. It breaks God's heart to see us so broken. God has forgiven him. Now it is time for your father to forgive himself, his friend, your mom, and his mom.

Many blessings to you and your family! Cheryl

Hi, Cheryl,

Yes, certainly, I will tell my story. God placed it in my heart to do so from the day I read your book. He told me that I would have to tell you my story, but I didn't truly understand. "Which story?" I asked. Then yesterday I felt very strongly that I needed to tell you about myself. Now you are asking me for my story. I'll get it to you as soon as I can, but please give me a few days.

My area of ministry is especially assigned to "Kingdom Relationships," particularly in the areas of family and business. God is guiding me and using you as a part of that.

Last year, He told me to establish a foundation, and He told me that He would provide mentors. This foundation will educate, train, and inspire parents to be leaders who take care of the inheritance that God has entrusted to them as stewards. You know that the whole world is groaning in expectation of the manifestation of the sons of God. The foundation is called Legacy International Foundation.

Blessings and Shalom and Love, Donell Knowles

Hi, Donell!

I just finished writing a story about a young lady who lived through her parents' anger and regrets related to their abortion and how she was put in the middle of that situation. I was wondering if you would like to share your feelings regarding the conflicts and sadness that were part of your parents' marriage and what it did to them and to you. I know it will stir up a lot of memories, but then you will be able to deal with them and find out how to be free from them.

I truly believe that it will help a lot of children who are living on the battlefield of their parents' lives. Please think about it; this also corresponds to your ministry to families and children. What about "us"? Is it our fault? Am I the problem, or is it them? These are questions that the kids are addressing within, and they don't know what to think or do. Hopefully, you will be one of the keys to help them.

Love, Cheryl

Hi, Cheryl!

I understand how you've been getting things together. I've been busy taking care of loose ends, too, and getting organized. I appreciate that God allowed me the time to do so, for it was very productive.

I believe that 2006 is going to be an awesome year in the Kingdom of God, because His warriors are starting to align themselves with His perfect purpose for their lives. As I start this journey of writing my life story, I am beginning now to recall an incident from my childhood that I had repressed and hidden deep within me.

The sense of freedom I'm experiencing is wonderful. When I first started thinking about the story, I had no emotion at all. Now I can't wait to see what else I will write. I now understand some things better about myself and my parents. You'll hear from me again soon.

Love, Donell

Hi Donell!

I'm looking forward to reading your story, because I know it will bring healing and understanding to you about your childhood and your parents. Then, when we see the overall picture with compassion and understanding...forgiveness and healing will begin, and I know it has already started in you.

Love, Cheryl

Dear Donell,

As I am reading your letter, I am weeping alongside the angels and rejoicing for your Mom, what a beautiful woman she was and her pain so deep. Thank you for sharing your stories which will touch the hearts of millions.

I look forward to your father's story. Together we will be able to unlock so many, many people who had no hope.

I love you my precious sister!

Cheryl

Don't Buy Into a Lie

DONELL'S MOM'S STORY

I was raised in a very strong religious environment. My mother tried to instill God's Word within us. She was faithful to send us to church with our grandmother every time the church doors opened if she was unable to attend. This was frequently the case because of her heavy work schedule, which involved her holding down three jobs to support her little family.

At the age of 19, after graduating from business school, mom married her childhood friend and sweetheart, my father, who was a professional musician at that time. Before long, mom found herself heartbroken and disappointed with her unfaithful and abusive husband.

At the age of 22, with three children in tow, she realized that her dreams for a happy family had been invaded by real life. What could she do? What were her options? To save her life, she had to get away.

She decided to flee to the United States in order to start a new life. She took my baby brother and left me with my dad, while leaving my other brother behind with her parents.

Being a very confident, educated, and skilled woman, she knew she could make it as a single parent with the help of the Lord. At the age of

24, mom became involved with a very influential, powerful, and affluent older man who, in the beginning, appeared to be very nice. She never realized that her dream for a better life was about to turn into a nightmare, however.

In the beginning this gentleman courted her, treated her like a queen, and lavished gifts upon her and showed her what the jet-set life was like. Then she discovered the truth—he wanted to control her completely. He was obsessed with her and believed that she was his property.

Even though my brother and I were on different islands he would take her to visit us every two weeks and charter a plane to take her back with him, usually staying no longer than one day. He said that she fitted all the characteristics of the woman he wanted to have children with. He also warned her that if she ever left him, he would hunt her down and find her and then kill her and her whole family. He took very good care of my mother, and she lacked nothing; in return, he wanted her to have his baby.

The conditions were simple: if she ever wanted to leave, she could, but only after having his baby or babies, and if she did decide to leave, then his own children would stay with him and she would never see them again.

After she refused to consent to his demands, he became embittered and angry. Then he became more obsessive and violent with her. He would offer her anything and everything she wanted, if she would just have his baby, but she refused. She said that he idolized her more than God, and she would not compete with God.

She knew she had to get out of this destructive relationship, but she was terrified and trapped. He insisted on sex almost every day. Even when she didn't want to have sex with him, he forced himself on her, for she was his "property" and he "owned" her. He was very suspicious of her and thought that she would secretly have an abortion if she ever got pregnant.

Each month he threatened her at gunpoint by reminding her that he would kill her and her little family if she ever went to the police. My mom began to plan her escape. She made several attempts to run away, but each time he would find her and drag her back. The consequences she suffered at his hands grew worse and the beatings increased. Whenever he would beat her, he'd pay his doctor friend off so there would be no record of the violent abuse.

She was terrified of him but was determined to escape.

Sensing this, he beefed up his surveillance on her, to the point of even going to the bathroom with her and checking her handbags to ensure that she had no abortion or birth-control pills. To make sure that mom got the message, he even put a gun in my baby brother's mouth while he was asleep in front of her and threatened to harm him if mom ever got pregnant and aborted the baby.

In time she did become pregnant, and she felt she had no other choice but to have a secret abortion. So she arranged for my baby brother to sleep over with some friends where he would be safe for a few days. Somehow her husband found out about the abortion before she could escape. Enraged and vengeful, he confronted her. She quickly denied it and pretended to be pregnant because she knew that he would otherwise search for my baby brother and hurt him.

Something unexpected happened the next day, and this gave her the opportunity to win freedom for her and her child. Her husband had an important business trip that he had to go on. Usually whenever he would travel, he would take her. This time he didn't, because she pretended to be having morning sickness due to her "pregnancy." Because he had her passport, he felt safe.

Prior to this she had confided in someone that her boyfriend didn't know to help arrange her escape by getting her a traveling document. Now, she was only waiting for the opportunity. On that fateful day she took the documents and left the United States to fly back home.

It was wonderful to have my mom back at home. I was only 7 years old at the time. She was free to love her children and make a brand-new start. She threw herself into working three jobs to support us. Her associates and family would check in on us whenever she worked nights.

Then, a year later, she received a disturbing call one night from the authorities. There was a private investigator from the United States who was looking for her and they wanted to know why. She finally told the police about her abusive relationship in America and about the threats that her boyfriend had made against her life if she were ever to leave him.

The police decided to maintain a watch over us. They would even take mom to her work, then pick her up and bring her home afterward. She would invite them to have supper with us because they would also protect us during the evenings. The police became our protectors and good friends, and we all felt safe.

Several months later, after all the fear and anxiety had died down, life became normal once again. All was quiet and routine, and the police were not needed anymore. One evening, during a family gathering, however, there was a loud knock on the door.

Mom cheerfully went to answer the door and when she opened it, she almost fainted. There *he* was! There was a smile on his face and a gun pointed at her belly. She gasped! The memories of his threats and the terror of the past flashed before her. He had come to kill her and her entire family. He was a man of his word, and he prided himself on keeping his promises, so there he was in living color and true to his spoken words.

She quickly and quietly stepped outside with him, begging and pleading. With so much activity and celebration going on inside the house, no one really took notice of what was happening, but I noticed her posture and ran outside to help.

He proceeded to grab me and held me hostage at gunpoint for a few minutes while she cried, begged, and pleaded for our lives. All he kept talking about was how much he wanted a baby from her, and how she had insulted and dishonored him by having an abortion. She had killed his child, his heir, his heart's desire. How angry he was at her for doing what she did to him! He could not forgive her.

Eventually my grandfather began looking for us. He peered through the living room window and saw with terror what was happening to his favorite child. In a panic that grew out of his concern for the life of his daughter and granddaughter, he alerted the police. The police showed up with all their weapons, and within moments a marksman was on the roof of a neighbor's house, and he was prepared to take the intruder out if he didn't drop his gun.

There was a standoff, as threats were being made to our lives and to his own life. After what seemed like a terrifying forever, and after much negotiating, they finally got him to drop his gun. They took us to safety, handcuffed him, and whisked him away. We never saw him again. He was extradited to the U.S.A. and banned from ever entering our country again.

By this time, all of us were crying, frightened, and trembling with disbelief at what had just taken place. Grandpa took us inside to a private room. He lovingly hugged us and told my mother that he had heard everything, assuring her that she did not need to explain anything to him. He told her that he loved her, that she must let go of the past, and get on with her life. He reassured her that her secret would be safe with him, because he knew that knowledge of the secret would have greatly upset her mother.

Mom didn't fear being disowned, but because of strict Christian beliefs, she could not face the disgrace it would bring. She felt that some sins, such as the sin of abortion, were worse than others. Mom was aware that she needed healing, but was too ashamed to tell anyone about the abortions. She did not want anyone to judge her for what seemed to be an almost-unpardonable sin. So she became a prisoner to the very thing she tried to hide.

She was locked up, bound, and isolated. This was her self-imposed prison sentence here on earth. It was her secret that only God knew about and her earthly father took to his grave. She believed and thought that I was too young to remember. After that horrible day, nobody ever made mention of it again. It was as if it never happened.

When mom was 31 and I was 13, her father died. At that point mom slipped into a deeper depression. Life became very overwhelming for her, and she couldn't get beyond her cold, dark dungeon of guilty and depressing thoughts and feelings. In fact, she overdosed a few times and credited her children for keeping her alive. I was very angry with mom, because I didn't and couldn't understand what was happening to her. I was only 13 when she started to lose her grip on life.

Looking back now, I realize that she was not as happy as she had pretended to be. There was always a look of sadness in her eyes. Mom could not and would not trust anyone again. The abortions had left her a victim, both dependent and insecure in personal relationships. She couldn't love because she couldn't love herself. She always seemed happy on the outside, but no one realized that alcohol had become a problem for her, because we didn't see her drink that often. She drank in secret so she could keep on smiling. She never drank in public places. When she drank a beer or had a glass of champagne at a family gathering, we noticed that she would become more bubbly. In secret, the alcohol was helping her numb and ease her pain, but it had become a vicious cycle that was destined to end her life prematurely. She would become constantly drunk late at night, then sleep it off to escape the pain and torment. By the time she had visitors the next day she would be sober again.

Occasionally, my mom sang this song to us: "Smile though your heart is breaking, smile though your dreams are shaken, it'll all seem worthwhile, if you just smile." Another one of her favorite songs was the hymn "Amazing Grace," and she seemed to love to sing it: "Amazing grace, how sweet the sound that saved a wretch like me; I once was lost but now I am found, was blind but now I see." Each time she would sing these words, tears would stream down her cheeks, and I would hold her and tell her how much I loved her, and I would ask her not to cry. Years later, I came to understand why her mind was so fixed on this hymn, this powerful song that she clutched so dearly to her heart until the day she died.

At age 50, her fragile body could not take another drop of alcohol. She had developed cirrhosis of the liver. It was the end of her life, and she preparing to meet her Creator. She was aware that her old companions—grief, pain, hurt, suffering, guilt, alcohol, and remorse—could not go with her on her final journey. She would have to leave them behind. This caused her to feel alone and she was afraid.

A few weeks before she died, with tears in her eyes, she told me, *"Baby, I want you to know that I have just rededicated my life to the Lord. I have wasted so much time in doing so. Today I am free. I can see all the tricks the devil has played in my life. I listened to the wrong voices. I suffered greatly, because I believed a lie. Please tell everyone for me that God loves them no matter what they've done. Don't believe a lie. Today I can now go on knowing that God has forgiven me, and I can rest in peace. Soon I will be in our Maker's loving arms. Baby, I love you so much, don't ever forget that."*

Praise God that she finally realized, after all those heart-breaking years, that you don't have to believe a lie.

Mom's choices had followed her around constantly. Hebrews 12:5 says: *"And you have forgotten that word of encouragement that addresses you as sons."* That's what had happened to my mother. She always focused on her mistakes. She had asked God to forgive her, but she didn't forgive herself. Unforgiveness had prevented her from fulfilling her purpose and her destiny. It had contaminated her present moments and bled into her future. She had so much potential, so much love, but she was so confused. Unforgiveness had affected her vision and altered her judgment.

> *Therefore, since we are surrounded by such a great cloud of witnesses, let us throw off everything that hinders and the sin that so easily entangles, and let us run with perseverance the race marked out for us. Let us fix our eyes on Jesus, the author and perfecter of our faith, who for the joy set before him endured the cross, scorning its shame, and sat down at the right hand of the throne of God. Consider Him who endured such opposition from sinful men, so that you will not grow weary and lose heart* (Hebrews 12:1-3).

When God decided to raise a nation He called for children to be born so that men could pass the covenant promise of God to their children. He operates on the earth through our seed. Therefore, we must deal with the issue of abortion in order to fulfill God's purpose on the earth.

> *Then the Lord said, "Shall I hide from Abraham what I am about to do? Abraham will surely become a great and powerful nation, and all nations on earth will be blessed through him. For I have chosen him, so that he will direct his children and his household after him to keep the way of the Lord by doing what is right and just, so that the Lord will bring about for Abraham what He has promised him"* (Genesis 18:17-19).

The whole world is groaning in earnest expectation of the manifestation of the sons of God—our covenant rights as heirs of God.

Cheryl, thank you for being silent no more; you have allowed me to share my experience as a result of my mother's choice of abortion.

Time to Exhale

The letters that follow are Donell's letters to her parents.

Dear Mom,

I heard your muffled cries and saw the deep sadness in your eyes. I saw your pain beneath your beautiful, smiling face. I never really under-stood all that you were feeling. I knew how much you loved your children and, perhaps under different circumstances, things might have been differ-ent. You did what you thought you had to do, so you made abortion your choice.

You always seemed so preoccupied and so far away in thought. It seemed as if you had something big on your mind that you could not share with us. As my friend Stephanie once said, "All losses bring great sorrow. It is the path to faith. Sorrow comes to give us perspective. It is often through great sadness that our true greatness emerges. The fruits of faith fall from the tree of sorrow."

Your self-condemnation cut you off from the life and purpose that God had for you. When you died, one caller expressed the sentiments of all who loved you: *"Today the sun won't even shine; it, too, seems to be mourning because a little light has left the world."*

Alcohol was the vehicle, but the choice of abortion was the seed of your demise. Its nutrients were despair, disappointment, sorrow, grief, and pain. The act of abortion was a temporary act that brought temporary relief from a situation that would soon cause a lifetime of pain. No one saw the root; we only saw the potential you had.

Your friends and longtime associates flew in to attend your funeral. There was so much love in the atmosphere that day. Our grief was padded by the love you gave to us and to others, as well. As we left the graveyard that afternoon, your beautiful 5-year-old granddaughter said, "Mommy, why are we leaving Grammy all alone in the big dark coffin?"

I sadly realized that you had entered a self-made coffin long ago. At the end of your sojourn on earth. However, God kept His promise, and He did not forsake you.

He said, *"Never will I leave you; never will I forsake you"* (Heb. 13:5).

You left me with loving brothers, and I am not alone. You left us with an admonition to live a godly life so we would see you once again in Heaven. This is the best legacy any parent can leave for their children. Thank you, mom, for your love which still holds and embraces us each day.

Your precious grandchildren wrote this just for you:

Like a candle you will always glow
Like a river you will always flow
Like a dove you left us with a sign of peace
You are trapped in our hearts and cannot be released.

We love you, mom!
Your loving daughter,
Donell

Dear Paps,

The years go by and with each passing day I grow to love and understand you more and more. I understand your pain. In ignorance you made some wrong choices. We all do. So please don't let it destroy your life.

Paps, I love you too much to watch you hurt. You have to decide to forgive yourself. God loves you and He has forgiven you. Please don't stay in this dark cycle of pain. It will break your spirit, paralyze you, and then wear you out. I know that mom has forgiven you. She really always wanted the best for you.

Do you remember the series of letters that mom wrote to you while she lay dying in the hospital? She wanted and needed to talk to you, because she wanted you to know that she forgave you. Paps, stop feeling sorry for yourself and regretting your past. It is over. It's done, it's gone, it's finished, and you are still here. It's time to come out of your dark cave and enjoy life once again.

God's plans for you are good, and they will never harm you. He will never allow you to be in a position that you can not get out of. Just trust Him and believe. It's time to put off the tired, sad, old man and become the new man that you were destined to become. There is so much potential within you.

God has confidence in you. Otherwise, He would not have allowed you to survive all the things He has brought you through. I agree with my friend Stephanie who said, "A good ending is one where we can believe. It is a seed of faith planted, and it is where hope begins."

Your life is not over; there is still so much living left to be done. God still has many blessings in store for you as soon as you get rid of the heavy burden you have been carrying by yourself. Just confess it and give it to Him!

God's yoke is easy and His burden is light. The Bible invites us to come unto God when we are heavily burdened and He will give us rest. In His Word God is constantly reminding us of His love and promises to us. He wants to encourage us, help us, and preserve us.

Please take God into all the spots in your life where you became bitter with yourself. There He will heal you, forgive you, restore you, and raise you back up to where you belong. He did it for me, and He will do the same for you.

God wants to hear you play your beautiful music once again and so do I! The world needs to be blessed once again with your beautiful gifts that our heavenly Father has bestowed on you.

Your loving daughter,

Donell

So in our love, understanding, and forgiveness of others we will release the rope of anger that has bound us within the cave of darkness and despair. To forgive is to love, and to love is to live. Today I can love you freely because I know I am loved and forgiven. Let God love you and forgive you, so that you too can be free to love and be loved.

As I come out of my dark cave and into the marvelous light, I will be bringing with me so many others who had once been locked and hidden in their caves but now can come out and start living once again. This is just like what happened to King David when he reclaimed his rightful inheritance after he had been running and living like an outlaw, and hiding in a cave from King Saul and his enemies.

David was finally rejoined with his family and friends once they knew where to find him. The Bible says: *"David left Gath and escaped to the cave of Adullam. When his brothers and his father's household heard about it, they went down to him there. All those who were in distress or in debt or discontented gathered around him, and he became their leader. About four hundred men were with him"* (1 Sam. 22:1-2).

And, as the story goes on, when David came out of the cave, he came out in strength and number. David was then able to pursue, conquer, and overtake everything that God had purposed for him. This is comparable to what God has planned and purposed for you. He will be faithful to complete and fulfill those plans and purposes in your life. He will do for you what He did for King David, and He will restore you to the Kingdom of God. If you believe, have faith, and are obedient to His Word, then God will help you to be victorious in every area of your life.

Rejoice. You are not alone, for Jesus lived and died for us so that we can go on living forever throughout all eternity with Him. May God's love richly bless you and bring you back into His loving arms.

The Kingdom of God is yours! Just believe, have faith, and know that He truly loves and forgives you!

Those Phantom Spirits

Have you ever had a feeling or a thought that seemingly came out of nowhere and made you feel extremely angry, sad, indifferent, or numb? This response could be triggered by a word, a city, a sight, a description, an odor, a conversation, a song, or by a movie or a TV program.

The anger, hatred, or sadness manifests itself, and you just don't quite know where it came from, and you cannot explain why you are feeling the way you do. It is as if someone hit you on the back of your head with a baseball bat, and, as you turned to see who did it, you discovered that no one was there. This is what I call a "phantom spirit." Such phantom spirits are thoughts that are deeply hidden within you, but they "jump out" from time to time to haunt and menace you.

First, let us define the word "phantom." *Webster's New World Dictionary* defines the word as:

1) Something that seems to appear to the sight but has no physical existence; apparition; vision; specter.

2) Something feared or dreaded.

3) Something that exists only in the mind; illusion.

4) A person or thing that is something in appearance but not in fact.

Now let us define the word "spirit." *Webster's* defines the word as:

1) The life principle, esp. in man, originally regarded as inherent in the breath or as infused by a deity; same as soul (sense).

2) The thinking, motivating feeling part of man, often as distinguished from the body, mind, intelligence.

3) Life, consciousness, thought, etc., regarded as separate from matter.

4) A supernatural being, esp. one thought of as haunting or possessing a person, house, etc.

5) An individual person or personality thought of as showing or having some specific quality.

6) A frame of mind; disposition; mood; temper.

So we can say that a spirit is a prevailing thought that could rule and reign over us and haunt us. What thoughts are ruling over your life? Are they thoughts of love, peace, and joy, or are they thoughts of anger, loss, unforgiveness, revenge, rejection, death, and/or abortion? These are feelings and emotions that are going to rule, reign, dominate, and menace your life, for as you think in your heart, so shall it be. (See Proverbs 23:7.) And, like a phantom, these spirits will appear and create havoc in your life, causing drama and misunderstanding all around you.

As I have been writing this book, God has been constantly guiding me to address issues that have laid hidden deep within me, inner conflicts I didn't even realize I had. For example, I had an issue with Las Vegas, yet I did not recognize my underlying hatred toward that city. Las Vegas—the convention city, the city of lights, excitement, entertainment, good food, and the city that doesn't sleep. It is the city that dazzles, mesmerizes, entices, seduces, and charms everyone. I had always wondered why I had such a dislike for Las Vegas. He revealed the answer to me in prayer.

God asked, *"Cheryl, do you know why you dislike Las Vegas so much?"*

I replied, "Yes, remember that one weekend when I went there and lost a lot of money? That is why."

I realized that I could have done a lot better with my hard-earned money, which I had left on the gambling table. Since that day, I have stopped gambling and really have never cared if I ever saw the city again.

You see, the bridal buyer convention is held there twice a year, and because I am in that business I am forced to go to Las Vegas, the city I remember and associate with monetary loss. In fact, every time I thought of Las Vegas I could only think of *huge* losses. I saw Las Vegas as a city that takes everything away from you. So, when friends and customers would find that I was going to Las Vegas, they would say, "Wow! That's exciting! Are you looking forward to it? What shows and restaurants do you go to? How fun!"

I would always grimace and reply, "I hate Las Vegas; I don't enjoy the city at all."

When I would go there for the conventions I would do what I had to do and leave immediately. I would actually feel angry about having to be there. My three days at the Las Vegas Bridal Show would consist of me working the convention from 8:30 A.M. to 6:30 P.M., then going to have a nice dinner, after which I would return to my room to go over what I'd seen and decide what my purchases for the next season would be.

I never had any interest in going to any of the highly acclaimed, star-studded productions and shows the city offers. I just couldn't enjoy the city. Those were my typical feelings and activities when I went to Las Vegas.

As I continued in prayer, I received quite a revelation. God asked me, *"Do you really know why you hate the city?"* He then asked me to look back at the time when I had lost so much money there and what exactly had happened that weekend.

As I reflected on that time, I remembered how horrible it was. Then it hit me! It was the weekend when I had my second abortion—and it had happened in Las Vegas! In my mind I had suppressed the memory of the abortion in order to protect myself from the sadness and depression that would come upon me when my thoughts would go in that direction. Obviously, that is why I had always associated Las Vegas with huge losses. I discovered it wasn't the large amount of wasted money that bothered me, for money can always be replaced. It was the loss of the precious life of my baby that can never be replaced, and my heart and soul continued to ache over that bad decision all through those years.

Yes, I experienced *a huge loss—the loss of a precious life that can never be replaced!*

"Cheryl," God said, *"you need to forgive both the doctor and the city for your great loss. I've forgiven you, now you need to forgive and let go of all the circumstances, locations, and people involved with your abortion."*

As I pondered this, I remembered I also had to forgive my friend who drove me there. He felt he was helping me, and all these years I had been mad at him and I really couldn't figure out why—until this new understanding came to me. Now I knew. It was because I had been mad at myself and at the entire situation, and unfortunately he was part of this sad situation in that he had driven me to Las Vegas. You see, our anger contaminates everything around us.

Excitedly, I called my friend Lornah to tell her of my new-found freedom. I explained to her about my breakthrough, my new understanding of the causes for my underlying hatred and anger toward Las Vegas. As I spoke, she grew silent.

Finally, she said, "Cheryl, thank you for setting me free. I now understand why I hated coming back to live in my mother's house after my divorce and why I hated the city of Long Beach, as well. I knew that I had forgiven my mother and had been reconciled to her, but there was an anger within me that I couldn't put my finger on.

"Now I know I need to forgive the house and the city where all my issues, bitterness, and unhappiness began. People used to ask me where I live, and I would say, 'Long Beach.' Typically they would reply, 'How beautiful!' My response, 'I hate Long Beach.' Now I know where this intense anger against the city is coming from. Thank you."

God is so good to us. Now we are both totally free! And in the same way He freed us, He will be faithful to His promise, and He will free you too!

God will leave no stone unturned in effecting our deliverance if we will allow Him to rule and reign over our lives. We must simply listen to Him as He speaks to us so that He can reveal the things that are hindering and blocking us. Don't be afraid to open the door to self-discovery, for in this discovery you will find your freedom. Yes, it will be initially painful for you to go through the deeply hidden issues, but in the end you'll find light at the entrance of the cave. As you emerge from your cave, you will find victory and total deliverance for your life.

What thoughts, feelings, and emotions have you been hiding? What are the phantom spirits that are hindering you from coming into the fullness of living? Do you remember in Chapter 6 how Jim talked about hating Wednesdays? Likewise, there is Regina's Story in Chapter 10. Do you remember how she spoke of not being able to enjoy life?

You need to address these areas of darkness that have been deeply hidden within you by taking the following steps:

1. Acknowledge the issue(s).
2. Confess and repent for the issue(s) and circumstances.
3. Forgive the issue(s) and everything connected with it/them (i.e. people, locations, cities, days, seasons, etc.).
4. Release them and let them all go.
5. Then, forgive yourself.
6. Ask Jesus to be the Lord of your life.

For the wages of sin is death, but the gift of God is eternal life in Christ Jesus our Lord (Romans 6:23).

And everyone who calls on the name of the Lord will be saved (Acts 2:21).

Once you have completed all these steps, you will come out of the dark, hidden cave of your life and enjoy the fullness of what God has planned and purposed for you.

So let us all have a "coming-out party" to celebrate our emergence from the darkness. What a mighty celebration this is going to be! I'll be looking for you there at the entrance to your cave, for that is the place where you will find me rejoicing and cheering you on!

With much love, peace, and happiness,

Cheryl

25

Our Testimony Is To Help One Another

We never realize what a person may be going through. However, God allows our paths to come together, to cross so that we can help and enrich each other's lives. Every person I have met throughout my life I will forever remember. Each encounter has become a jewel in my life and is stored in my memory bank. I have learned, discovered, and experienced so much from others, and I've learned that life is complex, multi-faceted, difficult, challenging, unique, and beautiful.

The wisdom and understanding that we attain as we go through difficult times should never be discounted; for your victories over certain situations will help bring another person to wholeness and victory in their circumstances and lives. Sometimes we just need to extend ourselves, to move out beyond our own selves in order to reach out to others so we can fulfill our purpose, which then becomes our testimony.

A month ago a business associate, Jason, walked into my store just to say hello. I hadn't seen him for over a year. He was the proud father of three little boys who were all under 5 years of age. He and his wife believed that their little family was complete. With the high cost of living, for them to have another child would be an added expense that they thought they could not afford.

As we talked and got caught up on what had been happening in our lives, I told him about the book I had just written and about the musical, as well. Then I went into the details of how my abortion had destroyed the relationship between me and my husband and how abortion is not a quick fix or solution to an accidental pregnancy. I shared that if men would just love their wives as Jesus loved His church then marriages would survive all circumstances.

I told Jason how Jesus laid down His life for His church and how He cherished and treasured her. I went on to explain that if husbands treated their wives with God's love, we would not have any more abortions. For some reason, I then suggested that Jason take a copy of my book and musical home with him to give to his wife.

A few weeks later, I saw Jason in the shop again. He said that he was sorry that his wife didn't get a chance to send a check to our foundation, but that he was there to give it to me personally. As he was writing out the check, I asked if she had read the book. He told me, "No, I haven't given it to her yet. We both have been so busy."

Then he quietly said, "The timing of you giving me that book and CD was pretty quirky. When I arrived home that evening, my wife hesitantly told me that we were positively pregnant with our fourth child. As I listened to her, I gently wrapped her in my arms and told her how much I loved her and how much I wanted our precious new baby."

Earlier that morning, he and his wife had gone to have her first sonogram. He proudly described how his precious little one was 4 centimeters long and how he is hoping for another little boy.

As he said that, I told him what I heard the Holy Spirit tell me: *"It is going to be a girl."*

He exclaimed, "That's great! I'm telling everyone I want a boy, but deep down I really want a little girl. Three boys are enough. I want a little princess now." Laughingly, I said, "Well, Jason, I heard *little girl*! So let me know the good news when you find out next month and I will rejoice along with you. We'll see how good my prophecy is."

He was so happy and excited, and I could see and feel his joy. God is so good to us!

Sometimes we wonder why we share our stories or sad tales with others, but it is because God wants us to impart an answer to a difficult problem that someone is going through. It could be your testimony that someone needs to hear in order to strengthen them or help them.

God used me this way one day in church. A woman was sitting in a pew and listening to my testimony. I could feel and see the sorrow that she held within. The pain, regret, and remorse that I shared with the audience were the very things she had been experiencing for the last 15 years of her life.

Her head was bent down, her shoulders hunched over as if she was trying to hide and shelter herself from the world, and her hands were fidgeting with a moist Kleenex as she wiped away her tears. My heart went out to her.

As she listened to my words, I gradually saw her lift up her downtrodden head in recognition of God's loving mercy. As my eyes caught hers, I saw a glimmer of hope shine through.

As I shared the good news of Jesus and His visitation in my life, I shared how He had forgiven me for every sin I committed when I confessed them to Him. I told the congregation that He had taken my sins upon Himself as He was on the cross. I assured them that He had forgiven me, and I told them how He had encouraged me to forgive myself. I explained that I had needed to forgive myself if I were ever to get past the very real pain that had come from the tragic and sad times of my life.

After hearing my testimony that lady walked home in victory, because she had released all of her life and concerns to God. She forgave every incident and every person that had done injustice or harm to her. Then she forgave herself. That very night the healing power of God's love descended upon her and she was completely healed from the daily severe migraine headaches that had been plaguing her for the last 15 years.

Two weeks later I saw her at another meeting. She thanked me for sharing my testimony, and she was beaming with joy. She excitedly told me that when she went up to the altar on that previous evening and gave everything to God, including her grief, sorrow, guilt, and shame, she felt cleansed and forgiven and she was able to forgive herself for her abortions.

She went on to tell me how her secret sins had kept her so locked up and in pain. They were secrets that she held so tightly within, things she had never shared with anyone. She was so happy to report that God had instantly healed her of her migraines.

She had been serving in the church for over seven years, and, as she did so, she had been trying to find resolutions for the issues of her life, but her thoughts and beliefs always dragged her down into the pit. Hers was a pain and guilt that she believed no one could ever forgive, but now she knew the truth and she was free at last!

As I shared my sad story and told of God's restoring and unconditional love, this lady was finally realized that God had forgiven her for the four abortions she had. Now she knew that we serve and have a wonderful, loving, restoring, and healing God who loves us so much that He willing gave His life to redeem us from our sins and transgressions and return us to His loving, restoring arms—back into the Kingdom of God where we belong!

Another example of the importance of our testimonies took place as I was sitting in a woman's office going over my account and my new orders with her company. I felt led to tell her about my book and the musical. As we talked, she commented to me how sad it must have been for me to have to go through such sad ordeals.

Then she mentioned three times how lucky she was to have never experienced an abortion. We talked for about for 45 minutes, then her personal secretary left the room to check on my orders. At that point she whispered to me, "I know how sad you must feel. I had an abortion when I was 19. My parents made me have it because they felt that the man I was dating was not right for me. Plus, being Asian, I couldn't disgrace them. Anyhow, I didn't want my secretary to know, because you know how people talk."

My heart went out to her. She had been hiding this secret sin within her all these years, and I was the first person with whom she was able to share it. For 17 sad years she had been holding this memory inside of her with all its accompanying pain, grief, and regret.

Such a secret continually haunts you and there seems to be no relief. As this woman slumped back against her chair, I heard a long sigh come from her, for she felt relieved that she had finally told someone after all those years. Now it was no longer a deep, horrible secret, for now it was out in the open, and she had found someone who would be compassionate with her in her anguish and guilt, someone who could identify with her and the pain that she had been experiencing.

I shared with her the Good News of Jesus, now it was up to her to accept God's forgiveness or reject it. Her dilemma was that she is a Muslim and her parents are very strict. They will not allow her to go to any Christian event. The traditions of her culture play a very significant role in her life.

I pray for her daily, asking God for her healing and her salvation.

26

With a Song in My Heart

ANATOMY OF A LOVE SONG

A dear friend of mine, who is a great songwriter, singer, and musician, came to see me one day. His name is Willie Tata. He is a minister of God, and he asked if I would like to hear a song that he wrote.

Because of my testimony that I shared in the church 18 years ago, Willie knew I would be able to do something with the song that he wrote in March 2000. He tried to sell it to some of the Pro-Life groups, but they told him, "Beautiful song. Thank you, but no thanks." He even sent it to the White House to see if President Bush would like to use it, and the response was the same.

In February 2001, Willie came to me and said, "Cheryl, I have a song for you. It is your song. I want you to consider buying it." As I listened to his song, I started to weep, and I knew that God had written this song for me. I told Willie that I would think about it and then took the song home to listen to it again. Every time I played it, I wept. There were still parts of me that had not been completely healed and God wanted to do a complete healing within me. Every time I played this song, it ministered to me.

A year later, I contacted Willie and told him I was interested in his song. I promised God that one day I would produce the song, never knowing the depths through which I would have to go. My education is in the field of pharmacology and my professional life has developed and evolved into business and management. I became a jeweler, then the owner of a bridal salon. What did I know about music?

First of all, I can barely sing on key. I can't read music, and I really can't play an instrument unless you consider playing "Chopsticks" on the piano a talent. I have never written a song before in my life. So what was I supposed to do with Willie's song?

In the following three years, God worked upon my heart and spirit to finish writing the book about my abortions. It was hard to do, for it brought forth too many sad memories. Finally, in obedience to the will of God, in the beginning of February 2005, I set out in earnest to finish my book.

I rewrote *Make Me Your Choice* and composed new parts for Willie's song, making it into a duet and expanding it to encompass the different reasons people have for making choices and giving a man's perspective, as well.

As I was working on the song, God also put into my heart the mission to write a musical play that is based on its message. The musical shares the experiences of various people who have made choices in their lives. Some chose abortion, others chose life.

The musical brings healing and restoration to all those who chose abortion; and it brings understanding and compassion to friends and families affected by their choice. It sheds light on the pain that abortion brings into people's lives and offers various alternatives. Also, it shows them that they are not alone.

They will see that the gift of life within them is our world's future hope, wealth, and its next generation. God told me, *"My love and My forgiveness are to shine forth along with My purpose for mankind."* Those were His instructions to me.

In 2002, God placed a plan inside of me to establish a foundation called the DreamSeeker/StarMaker Foundation. Through the foundation I am to offer scholarships to teenagers who are interested in the fine arts.

Our vision is to help our youths achieve in life and to teach them how to discover and fine-tune their God-given potential and giftings. The foundation's purpose is to help develop young people in the fine arts, performing arts, creative arts, business, education, or whatever else they may put their hands and minds to do through free seminars, mentoring, and scholarships.

Our goal is to teach this generation about God and what He wants for them in life, to teach them to transform challenges into victories, problems into solutions, questions into answers, and giftings into God's perfection for their lives. With God, nothing is impossible to those who believe and persevere, to those who seek the Spirit of God's excellence to come upon their lives.

DreamSeeker/StarMaker is reaching out to young people who are interested in fashion, music, the creative arts, leadership, business, and scholastic achievement through our scholarship programs so that we can make a difference in their lives today, for they are all made with a purpose, designed by God to be our future hope and our next generation of leaders and teachers.

Our mission statement underscores the idea that God has created each and every one of us for a specific purpose, and with creative talents that will affect mankind. Once we are tapped into God, we will experience His Presence and His will, and once we understand God's purpose and incorporate His principles into our lives, we will become victorious in all that we do.

God created me with creative gifts which I didn't even realize or know existed until I tapped into His Presence and His redeeming love. It was then I understood His plan and purpose for my life. All along I never realized how valuable my life was and how each of our lives are testimonies to His plan for mankind.

I am not a mistake, nor an accident. I was put here on earth for a specific purpose and a specific reason. My life is not random. So, as I re-surrendered my life totally back to God, He told me of the great purpose He wanted me to share with the world.

I have come to sense His broken heart as He looks upon this earth and mankind from His throne in the heavens. He is hurt by the mass genocide of His future hope and legacy for the future of mankind. He is saddened that we have become so casual and numb with regard to the destruction of His precious gifts to the world and that we have become a world that has looked down upon His creation with such shallow, selfish, callous, and ignorant hearts—with a total lack of understanding of His purpose and destiny.

I felt His heart reach out to me: *"I want you, Cheryl, to bring understanding and hope to a lost and dying generation, one that does not understand the value of My greatest and most beautiful creation: Man and has failed to realize My purpose for all of mankind. The beauty that is within them, the beauty that is within my precious daughters' wombs—that beauty is the gift of life and hope for a future generation.*

"I have sadly watched as men and women, politicians, world governments, and misguided people have destroyed and killed my future leaders, teachers, inventors, businesspeople, inventors, ministers, and scientists, people who would have had the cure for various diseases. This has happened all because of a lack of understanding, fear, selfishness, power, and greed. They are not just destroying a blob of tissue. They are destroying the answers and solutions to mankind's problems that I had placed in these babies that were unfortunately aborted.

"So that is why in some cases that new inventions, solutions to the horrible problems that the world is facing, and new cures for cancer and other diseases remain undiscovered; it's because the ones who had these answers came back to heaven too quickly. They were aborted, and the babies were not able to finish out their assignments on earth that I had purposed for them to carry out in the world. Now the people will have to wait a little longer for the answers. They have ignorantly aborted their solutions too many times!"

May God's love song, musical, and book minister to you and touch your heart and soul. May they bring you back from the cave of darkness into the loving arms and marvelous light of your heavenly Father.

All proceeds from the sale of this book and musical will go back into the foundation to help provide scholarships, promote abortion awareness, and to take the musical globally so everyone will gain understanding and insight into the problems of abortion and understand God's redeeming love and His beautiful grace.

Please help us get this timely project into the public schools, the prisons, the churches, and to all the cities and nations. Write or e-mail us to find out when the musical will be coming to your area, where it will be playing next, or to see my speaking itinerary. I am looking forward to meeting and seeing you!

Love and Blessings,

Cheryl

EPILOGUE
Thirty-six Years of Silence Finally Broken

After that day when we had the abortion of our baby we never once discussed or mentioned it again. After 36 years of silence, repression, and secret pain prevailed over our lives…I was finally able to break the silence that had kept both of us hostage and apart.

It was Easter Sunday 2006 and we just had a beautiful Easter family dinner party at my son's home. God had put it on my heart that what better day than Easter to present my ex-husband with my book.

As we all walked out the door saying our good byes to each other, I asked John if I could speak to him before he left. As we were walking toward our cars, I shared with him how I had just written a book called *Make Me Your Choice* about abortion and how it affected our lives.

He replied, "Oh, that's good."

As I handed him the book and music CD I continued on and said, "It's been a long and hard journey to write this book, but in writing it, it has brought me complete healing, great peace, wholeness, and God's forgiveness. I pray that this book will do the same for you."

As I got into my car, tears of joy and love started to stream down by face as I thought, *"Yes John, it is finally time to exhale."*

Thirty six years of silence was now broken, and the darkness is now pierced with love, understanding, and forgiveness as John, the children, and I all move into God's marvelous light...*free at last.*

Is there a painful silence that has separated you from loved ones, family members and friends?

If so, I pray that you will find the courage to break the silence and pierce it with love, truth, understanding, compassion, and forgiveness. Only then can we move into God's marvelous light and beautiful purpose for our lives. Remember, I am here at the entrance of your cave as you come into His marvelous light. There you will find me cheering you on to victory and encouraging you to fulfill your God-given purpose and destiny!

Special Acknowledgements and Thank You

A special "Thank You" to all who participated in making God's project and this book possible. To all the brave ladies and men who shared their heart and pain.

To Dr. Myles Munroe, my mentor, friend, and Pastor who inspired and encouraged me to maximize and fulfill the purpose and destiny God has called me to. To my friend, Sherwood Jones, who helped with the editing of my book and is the director of the musical.

To Pastor Jimmy MacDonald, music director of the musical, and music and sound engineer for the CD. To Consuelo Peterson, Rose Lawson, Eileen Coyle, Jimmy MacDonald, and Willie Tata for their beautiful music and songs.

To Yoly Tolentino, Joyce Cronin, Cassidy Parnell, Eileen Coyle, Mone Yaa Oppong, Rose Lawson, Lisa Houston, Pastor Reggie Smith, Pastor Jimmy MacDonald, and Sherwood Jones for their talented voices. To Chandra Hope for the heartfelt *"Make Me Your Choice"* music video.

To my four greatest cheerleaders, my children, John, David, Mark, and Stephanie who are my heart. And to my Mom, Dad, and Uncle Walter who always loved and believed in me. To my dear friend and mentor, Ernie Bubsy, who never stopped believing in me.

Thank you for being His hands extended here on earth, you have all greatly enriched and blessed my heart.

I love you all!

DreamSeeker/StarMaker Foundation is currently producing a beautiful musical called *"Make Me Your Choice"* which debuted it's theme song in the Bahamas at the International Third World Leadership Association Conference in November 2005 where it got a standing ovation. This musical shares the lives of various people who have made a choice in their life... some chose abortion, others chose life. This musical will bring healing and restoration to all those who chose abortion, and will bring understanding and compassion to why they did. God's love and forgiveness shines forth.

We pray that this musical brings to light the pain that abortion causes in people's lives and helps them realize that there are other alternatives available . . . and that they are not alone. The Gift of Life within them is our world's future hope and wealth, our next generation!

In adition to this book, a *"Make Me Your Choice"* music CD is also available. If you would like to order this for your bookstore please call the number below or e-mail us.

To book this musical in your church, please contact:

DreamSeeker/StarMaker Foundation

Telephone: 714-713-4400

E-mail: Makeme-yourchoice@sbcglobal.net

GRANDMA JOY'S HOPE FOR HURTING WOMEN

This book is filled with real-life personal stories, testimonies, prayers, scriptures, and answers to help women find wisdom, strength and salvation. Each thought-provoking story is concluded with a light-hearted story providing readers with lots of laughter.

ISBN 0-7684-2351-1

Available at your local Christian bookstore.